The Agile Manager's Guide To

MANAGING
IRRITATING PEOPLE

The Agile Manager's Guide To

MANAGING IRRITATING PEOPLE

By Joseph T. Straub

Velocity Business Publishing
Bristol, Vermont USA

For Pat and Stacey

Copyright © 1999 by Joseph T. Straub

All Rights Reserved

Printed in the United States of America

Library of Congress Catalog Card Number 99-64994

ISBN 1-58099-017-7

Title page illustration by Elayne Sears

Second printing, October 2000

If you'd like additional copies of this book or a catalog of books in the Agile Manager Series™, please get in touch.

- **Write us:**
  Velocity Business Publishing, Inc.
  15 Main Street
  Bristol, VT 05443 USA

- **Call us:**
  1-888-805-8600 in North America (toll-free)
  1-802-453-6669 from all other countries

- **Fax us:**
  1-802-453-2164

- **E-mail us:**
  info@agilemanager.com

- **Visit our Web site:**
  www.agilemanager.com

The Web site contains much of interest to business people—tips and techniques, business news, links to valuable sites, and electronic versions of titles in the Agile Manager Series.

Contents

Books in the Agile Manager Series™:

Introduction

"My job would be great if it weren't for the people." How many times have you said that? Quite a few, probably. And you're not alone. The trouble is, you can't dictate how your peers or your bosses behave toward you. Nor can you mandate your subordinates' behavior—even though you may have the power to hire and fire them.

This Agile Manager's Guide will give you some practical strategies and tactics for handling people whom you hate to work with but can't work without. Think of it as a survival guide and a compass that points the way to the executive suite. And why not? Your daily success—not to mention your annual performance evaluation—hinges on your prowess in getting over, under, around, or through many human roadblocks.

This isn't to imply, however, that every day is going to test your sanity or that all the people you work with will be cantankerous or unpleasant. In fact, if you *don't* believe that most coworkers will be compatible with and try to do right by you, life at work is really going to be miserable. But because sour apples are a workplace reality (albeit, thank goodness, a small minority), every manager needs to know how to deal with them positively.

Your goal in doing so, by the way, may be threefold:

- To make them more productive and useful to your company.
- To eliminate or reduce whatever obstacles they pose to your own success and peace of mind at work.
- To help some of them—especially those who report to you—change counterproductive behavior that may be retarding their success, limiting their advancement, and making them their own worst enemies.

Changing people's behavior or channeling it in more productive directions is no simple task, of course. In fact, most difficult people are like lobsters in a grocery-store tank. They are self-centered, work at cross-purposes, use each other as stepping stones, fight among themselves much of the time, sulk in corners when they don't, and thrash around with no regard for their colleagues. Nevertheless, you're stuck with them for now, and you can't let them jeopardize your success.

The Agile Manager's Guide to Managing Irritating People will help you step back, calm down, assess fractious folks fairly, and devise ways to deal with them effectively despite their exasperating nature. And the techniques in this book will help you deal not only with the people who work for you, but also with peers and even bosses.

In short, it'll help you do your job while keeping irritating co-workers from doing you in.

The Agile Manager's Guide To

MANAGING
IRRITATING PEOPLE

Chapter One

Define 'Irritating' Productively

"Given a conflict, Murphy's law supersedes Newton's."

ANONYMOUS

*"I guess there are two schools of thought about this—
yours and mine."*

ERNEST GALLO, CEO, GALLO WINERIES

The Agile Manager slammed his door shut. His assistant, Steve, looked startled. Wow, he thought. Something's up. He almost never loses his cool.

In his office, the Agile Manager paced back and forth. He'd just found out an important new project would be delayed for a week, mainly because a key engineer had decided to go off on a speculative tangent that ended up bearing no fruit.

Idiot, he thought. What am I supposed to tell Don? He'll blame me for not checking in sooner. He replayed the scene in his mind one more time.

" . . . and you spent sixty hours on that?!"

"Yes," said Phil, the engineer, entirely at ease with himself. "I

11

thought it might yield some useful insights." His manner seemed designed to challenge the Agile Manager.

Ever since he won that industry design award, the Agile Manager thought to himself, he's been full of himself. He's become a know-it-all. Aloud he said, "But it cost us a week."

"I'm sorry," said Phil, stifling a yawn.

At that, the Agile Manager turned on his heel and left.

"Bad attitude," the Agile Manager muttered to himself as he walked down the hall. But when he heard himself say "attitude," he was reminded of a favorite line of his favorite boss, now long retired, Dick Jonas: "No bad attitudes. Only bad behaviors." Whether true or not, Jonas would tell him, behavior is the only thing we can get our hands on.

"OK, then, Mr. Phil," the Agile Manager said resolutely, "I'll get my hands on your behavior and give you a quick turn in a new direction."

Irritating people . . . hard to live with 'em; illegal to kill 'em. Some folks can irritate you just by breathing the same air.

So what to do? You must manage them. And that's just what this book will show you how to do.

Irritating people can be compared to lots of things, none of them pleasant. They're the interpersonal version of athlete's foot, but more aggravating to cope with. (You can soak your irritated feet in a bucket. Too bad you can't soak irritating people in that same bucket—head first.)

We tend to think of annoying people in unflattering terms, and maybe a little venting might be good for your soul here. Let's let it rip! Irritating people are:

- A burr under your saddle
- A Band-Aid floating in life's punch bowl
- Steel wool in the jockstrap of tranquillity
- Speed bumps on your road to success
- Thorns in your bed of roses
- . . . and the poison ivy in your Field of Dreams.

In short, they're nagging reminders that it's not a perfect world.

Yet as Ben Franklin said, "The Constitution only guarantees American people the right to pursue happiness. You have to catch it yourself." One way to do that is to learn to manage—and cope with—irritating people.

Understand That 'Irritating' Is a Subjective Term

But hold on a minute. To paraphrase the words of one U.S. president, "How do you define 'irritating'?" Just trying to do so can be, well, an irritating experience. Lots of things can cause us to brand people "irritating." To list a few:

Personality differences. Introverts may frustrate extroverts; extroverts may annoy introverts. Some folks are as raucous as Robin Williams on a roll, while others, reclusive as hermit crabs, almost scuttle under the conference table during meetings.

Points of view or goals that clash with your own. Wouldn't it be a great world if everybody was reasonable—and did things your way?

Remember that most irritating people believe their behavior is reasonable and acceptable. Just ask them!

Conflicting priorities. You've asked Smedley to complete the budget estimates by 5:00, but Smedley pitches a fit. She's planned to work all afternoon on the McGregor proposal, then meet her sorority sister for a drink at 4:30.

Diverse backgrounds, experiences, lifestyles, and interests. If you could somehow draw a diagram of how all of these factors connect (or conflict) among the people in your work group, it'd give you nightmares. Don't go there! Let's just say that today's tossed-salad workplace sometimes gives managers indigestion when they try to mix all the ingredients together.

The strength of convictions and how they're expressed. Some of your colleagues may speak passionately about their work; others may speak passionately about their co-workers (which

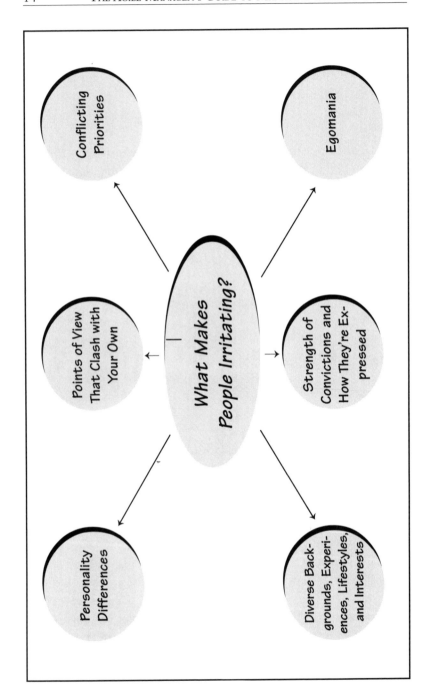

can get them in a heap of trouble if they're not careful). A few employees may come across as lively debaters to one boss, while another might declare them insubordinate and threaten to fire them. Some employees don't hesitate to give you a piece of their minds, while others need all the brain cells they've got just to get to work on time every day.

Egomania. Prima donnas who have racked up an impressive track record may become legends in their own minds. Their heads are so large they have to buy custom-made hats, and they fantasize that God often speaks to them—when He needs advice. (Does this sound like your doctor, lawyer, or that hotshot MBA down the hall? Aha!) But then, such folks *do* have the confidence of precedent behind them. As Dizzy Dean said, "It ain't bragging if you can back it up."

Watch out for prima donnas. Among the most irritating of people, they have become legends in their own minds.

So "irritating" seems to be a pretty subjective term. If you're looking for a pat definition, you won't find it here. And let's not use "irritating" as a synonym for "bad." Some excellent actors and actresses have been labeled "irritating" or "difficult to work with" just because they had no patience with flaky co-stars, inept directors, faulty lighting, or poorly written scripts. Sometimes that word "irritating" may also mean "honest," "an independent thinker," "self-confident," "forthright," or "not willing to put up with BS."

Who's Irritating Whom?

While we're at it, let's also admit that lots of so-called irritating people may think they're being perfectly reasonable. Of course they are . . . from *their* point of view. Just like the doting mother who whispered at her kid's graduation, "Why is everybody out of step with Johnny?," it's sometimes a matter of perspective.

We tend to force people into our own frame of reference whether they fit very well or not. Consider the tailor who traveled to Rome and got an audience with the Pope. When a friend asked what the Pope was like, the tailor said, "He was about a 42 regular."

You've also probably noticed too that people who are overloaded with pressure or problems (either on or off the job) can suddenly become irritable, blow hot and cold, and display bizarre behavior that may be very out of character for them.

Some teachers, for example, confirm that obnoxious behavior by kids who are normally well behaved usually signals problems at home. The same may be true for adult co-workers, who may be on the verge of "going postal" because of off-the-job troubles. In such cases, you may have to take control, step into the breach, and say, "Hey, you! I'm sorry about your personal problems, but I want you to drop your Uzi and get off that verge right *now!*"

No matter the source of the irritation, or how you characterize it, you still need to deal with it. After all, the irritation is impeding your on-the-job enjoyment and productivity.

Avoid the 'A' Word

Before we start in on techniques to do that, let's address a particularly important issue.

What "A word" do people often use when discussing irritating people? No, not *that* one. The other one: *Attitude.*

Let's not use it too often, though. "Attitude" is too darn vague. It's a convenient excuse to avoid describing the irritating person's behavior clearly. "I don't like her attitude" is about as precise a comment as "I don't like her hairstyle" or "He wears funny-looking shoes."

Let's substitute the word "behavior" instead, because behavior can be observed and recorded, while attitude, like beauty, tends to be in the eye of the beholder. How we perceive or interpret someone's attitude depends on our own background, experience, priorities, and prejudices.

Most of us have been snowed by somebody with a "great attitude" at one time or another, only to find that the person was all show and no go—or at least didn't go as far or do things as well as they'd led us to believe. When all the dust cleared, their behavior contradicted their rah-rah, gung-ho attitude.

I had one partner like that on a book project. It was a shotgun wedding; we hadn't met until the editor threw us together. The other fellow dressed sharp, acted sharp, threw around all the right buzz words, and oozed "just you 'n me baby" "we're gonna be a great team" one hundred-watt enthusiasm.

But when I mailed him about thirty pounds of up-to-date material that I'd cataloged for reference or to be used as examples (all of it related to his part of the project), he never bothered to open the darned cartons. His final product was much poorer for it. I suspected all along that the guy was more talk than action, and his returning those cartons unopened proved it.

Best Tip

Forget about 'attitude.' Instead, focus on behavior. It's the only thing you can identify and—hopefully—change.

Create a Plan

Okay, so you have an irritating person you need to deal with. In some cases, you can do it on the fly, because some people take criticism well, and one broad hint may be enough to settle the issue. If that's the case, congratulations.

Usually, you won't be so lucky. With most others, you'll need a plan to deal with the person or the irritation will continue. Forever. So here's a five-step plan that includes taking notes and spelling out the exact nature and extent of the irritation, speculating on its cause, clarifying how the person's behavior needs to change, classifying the irritating person, and choosing one or more management techniques that may work for people in that particular classification.

1. If somebody's behavior gets your knickers in a twist, start by summarizing it on paper in a sentence or two.

- How and to what degree is the behavior affecting you? Is it seriously impairing your performance or reputation? Derailing your train of thought? Causing you to lose sleep or make mistakes? Aggravating you so much that your productivity suffers?

- Exactly what is this person doing to make your radiator boil? Consider keeping an informal log for several days to help you identify consistent patterns. Ask such questions as:

  —What specific comments, conduct, or mannerisms do I find especially bothersome?

  —In what situations do these incidents usually occur? (One particular time of the day or month? During a crisis? When I'm extremely busy or working under a tight deadline? When I've had to refuse this person's request or assert my authority?)

  —Does the setting itself seem to trigger irritating behavior? Does this person usually provoke me when we're working one-on-one? As members of a group? In the presence of other subordinates? When we're in the company of higher-ranking colleagues such as my boss?

  —What state of mind was I in at the time? Was I feeling upset, angry, or anxious about something else when each incident occurred? Might I have felt less irritated if I had been feeling differently?

This record is more precise than merely trusting the incidents to memory. You need specific information to nail down the behavior's nature, circumstances, and possible cause. Why? Because you may decide to discuss the matter frankly with the irksome person, and if you do, you shouldn't talk off the top of

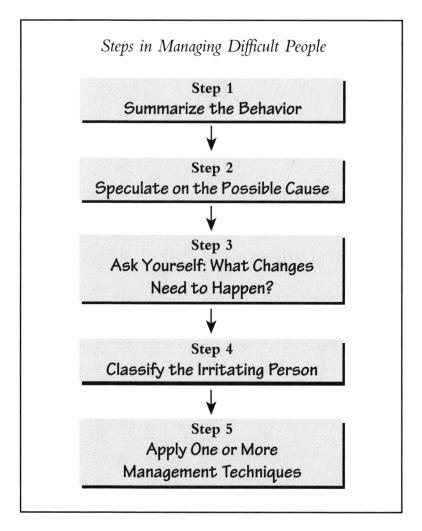

Steps in Managing Difficult People

Step 1
Summarize the Behavior

↓

Step 2
Speculate on the Possible Cause

↓

Step 3
Ask Yourself: What Changes
Need to Happen?

↓

Step 4
Classify the Irritating Person

↓

Step 5
Apply One or More
Management Techniques

your head or speak in generalities. Armed with details, you can state your case clearly and rationally and provide dates, times, and places where the bothersome behavior occurred.

Don't use the information as a "hit list," of course. Rather, create a record of specific behavior or remarks that rubbed you the wrong way, where the two of you were at the time, and your particular state of mind at the moment. Reviewing this information may help you analyze it more thoroughly and place it in better perspective as you move on through the next steps.

2. Speculate on the possible cause. Is there something you might do to eliminate or alleviate it? Is it possible that *you* could be the cause? (This shocking idea, farfetched though it may seem, will be discussed later in the book.)

3. Ask yourself what changes need to happen for the two of you to have a positive, constructive working relationship. Jot this information down on paper—don't just let it rattle around in your head.

4. Classify the irritating person according to the types discussed in chapter two or chapter three. Which description seems to fit best?

5. Select and apply one or more management techniques from step four's classification.

WHO'S THE IRRITANT?

Your choice of these techniques will depend, of course, on whether the irritating person is your boss, a peer, or a subordinate.

Here's a checklist of questions to help you put your relationship with each one in sharper focus.

If It's Your Boss

1. How valuable are you to your department and your overall organization? If you're the only one who does what you do and you do it well, you may be able to carry off even a major confrontation with your boss if it's necessary. But if you're not indispensable, tread lightly.

2. Do you have any advocates in higher management who would go to bat to save your job if your approach fails and your boss tries to carry out a vendetta against you?

3. How much does your boss count on you to cover for him? The better you make him look, the less risky it may be to speak candidly and deal with the situation head-on. A boss who can't afford to lose you has more reason to react positively to your plan.

4. What's the general health of your present relationship?

Peaceful coexistence? Armed truce? Occasional skirmish? Constantly at each other's throats? This can influence how tactful your approach should be and how you'll launch it.

5. Do you pose a threat to your boss's job or make him or her feel insecure or inept (perhaps because you have more education, experience, people skills, etc.)? If so, let diplomacy be your watchword. Antagonizing an already jealous or resentful boss is like playing Russian roulette with a bazooka.

6. What's the likelihood that your boss may move on, up, or out sometime soon? If a move is pending, you might be wise just to bide your time and do nothing until the problem goes away.

7. How sound have your performance evaluations been during the last few years? If they're outstanding, they may give you some measure of protection if your boss reacts badly.

8. How's the state of the job market? Are your skills and job knowledge relatively portable, flexible, up-to-date, and in demand? For example, a manufacturing production manager may have fewer employment options than an accountant, and a geographic information systems analyst may be hotter property than a procurement agent for a defense contractor. If things blow up and you become a casualty instead of a survivor, how easy will it be to land on your feet?

Each of these questions can help you decide how aggressive to be and how far out on a limb you can safely go. When the irritating person is your boss, perhaps the main thing to remember is this: Don't push an advantage unless you have it!

If It's a Peer

1. How much do you rely on this person for cooperation or information you need to do your job? If he or she has a major influence on your success, try to preserve a good relationship at all costs.

2. How much does this person depend on *you* for cooperation or information? The more reliant he or she is on you, the

greater the vested interest in keeping on your good side.

3. How much seniority does each of you have? The one who knows where the most bodies are buried has the most informal power.

4. Have the two of you crossed swords before? If so, what did you learn from that experience? If not, tactfully pick the brains of others who have had run-ins with this person. They might tell you what response to expect.

5. If you both report to the same boss, how does your relative influence with your boss compare? The more clout you have with your mutual manager, the more reason your peer should have to try to work compatibly with you.

If It's a Subordinate

Many of the questions you should ask here are the same ones to ask if the person was your boss—only now your roles are reversed.

1. How valuable is this person to your department and your overall organization? You may need to be more tactful with an indispensable employee than with one who's easy to replace.

2. Does this worker have Godfather-like friends or relatives in high places who might cause you problems if the two of you have a major conflict? (While you shouldn't let a well-connected employee make your work life unpleasant, it's important to identify which senior managers the employee might ask to pressure or intimidate you. That keeps you from being blindsided.)

3. How much do you rely on this worker's experience and skills? If you're new to the organization, an experienced employee can be a valuable ally and informal mentor until you get your feet on the ground and figure out the lay of the land. But if your approach to managing such an irritating person fails and the employee either turns against you or gets mad and quits, would that create major problems for you?

4. What's the likelihood that the employee may resign or retire soon? If you're patient, the problem may simply walk out

the door and not come back.

It goes without saying, of course, that you have formal authority over this person, which implies (but by no means assures) that he or she should appreciate the realities of your relationship and not rub you the wrong way. You have discretion over performance evaluations, pay increases and other rewards, recognition, job assignments, and delegated assignments that could make the employee's life either

Make sure of your value to the organization—or of your marketability—before taking on an irritating boss.

pleasant or miserable (not that you'd be a small enough person to do so, of course). Nevertheless, the power is there, and it should be acknowledged occasionally—if only during the employee's annual performance evaluation.

Some Parting Thoughts

Before we move on to meet our gang of repugnant personnel, it's important to remember four key points.

- Some people are weird, and they're weird for a host of reasons. Trying to figure out why may make you behave a little strange yourself, and it's fruitless, because you'll probably never figure them out. Just accept the fact that they are the way they are, and don't try to play amateur psychologist with them. That might be both legally and physically risky. As a manager, your main concern is to get them to work and relate to you and each other productively by managing their behavior as astutely as possible. That's the whole point of this book. It's not necessary to "understand" them, and there's no reason to beat yourself up if you don't.

- Don't wield your authority as a club when you're managing the irritating folks who report to you. It's a lot easier to get people to do things by using street smarts and persuasion than by waving your authority in their faces. Some of them won't be very impressed anyway. For more on that fact of life, talk to any cop. No, this book emphasizes *managing* irritating people, not bashing them into submission. Use your official power as the boss as a last resort—if at all.

■ Realize that some people's irritating behavior may be a symptom of mental illness, which is now protected by the Americans with Disabilities Act. Overreacting with such folks may bring on a messy lawsuit.

■ Last but far from least, some irritating people, to put it kindly, may not have all their corn flakes in one box. If that's the case, they could be just a minor incident away from violence, and that's nothing to mess around with. If you suspect someone is truly psychotic, talk to your boss or HR people about how to handle the situation. Don't be a hero.

The Agile Manager's Checklist

✔ Expect to encounter irritating people in the workplace. That way, the experience won't be as much of a shock.

✔ Understand that people usually believe it's the *other* person who's being aggravating or unreasonable.

✔ Substitute the word "behavior" for "attitude." Behavior is tangible and much easier to describe.

✔ Describe precisely how and to what degree the person's behavior is affecting you.

✔ Be willing to admit that you might be at least partly at fault for the situation.

✔ Spell out what changes must happen to create a productive working relationship with the irritating person.

Chapter Two

Types of Irritating People: Personalities

"He (or she) who angers you conquers you."

ELIZABETH KENNY

"All the strategic planning, financial rejiggering, and number crunching in the world won't help if it can't succeed in changing human behavior. And that, it seems, is the hardest thing of all to do."

SARAH BARTLETT, BUSINESS WRITER

Phil was holding court in the break room as the Agile Manager walked in. He leaned against a wall near the door, staring at Phil's back, listening. The two people facing him looked alarmed but didn't say anything.

" . . . I don't see why that deadline is so important," Phil droned. "I heard from a guy I know at headquarters that the second half of the project won't be funded until the next fiscal year anyway. Besides, I know I can improve it if I'm given half a chance. The boss

lacks a certain, ah, how to put it, flair." The two people looked at the Agile Manager with something akin to fear on their faces. He suddenly walked further into the room as though just arriving and said, "Hi everybody. Hey, did you hear that the manufacturing division's softball team won the Corporate League championship? Bloomie hit two homers. Phil, can you stop by my office later this afternoon? I want to go over some specs with you."

"Sure thing," he said blandly. Then he got up to leave, brushing by the Agile Manager without making eye contact.

One of the other people in the room, Anita, the leader of the design team, stayed back with the Agile Manager.

"He's getting to be intolerable," she said after the room had cleared. "I'm having trouble keeping him on task, and when I try to redirect him he brushes me off with a smirk like I'm his little sister asking him to help set the table or something. I know I'm team leader, but I don't have the power to discipline him."

"I know," said the Agile Manager. "This is something I have to take care of. Hey, I heard your diligence bought us back another couple of days on the project. How'd you do it?"

"Well, I came in over the weekend and . . ."

Some types of irritating behavior can stem from traits that seem to be woven into people's personalities. Then again, maybe their mothers were frightened by pygmy giraffes before they were born.

For whatever reason (and since this isn't a psychological textbook, thank goodness) let's just say, to paraphrase Popeye the Sailor, "they are what they are" both on and off the job: equal opportunity irritants who aggravate friends, family members, and co-workers alike. No playing favorites for them!

Now fasten your safety belts and keep your arms and legs inside the car as we begin our trip through this rogues' gallery of exasperation and provocation. When you come to a personality type that yanks your chain fairly often, slow down or stop for a while. You'll learn a few tips and techniques to help you manage the irritant.

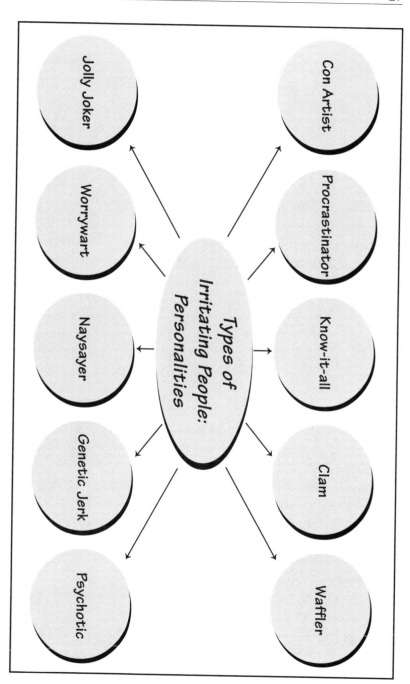

THE CON ARTIST

"You can get by on charm for about fifteen minutes.
After that, you'd better know something."

ANONYMOUS

Con artists may cozy up to you like a wet dog to a hot stove—but let's hope they smell a little better. Texans sometimes describe them as "big hat/no cattle." Others may call them phonies or BSers.

Although these folks usually report to you, they may also be your peers. Some of the more common types of con artists are:

Guilt-trippers. Guilt-trippers try to rattle a new or newly promoted boss's confidence with remarks like, "Our old boss wasn't like that," or "You do things different from every other boss we've had." Their strategy? To make you question your own judgment, worry about being accepted by your new work group, and fret more about being liked than about doing your job. By throwing you off your stride, guilt-trippers hope to make you reluctant to set and hold them to challenging performance standards.

Best Tip
Analyze and categorize con artists first. This helps you develop a clearer strategy for managing them.

The perpetually overstressed. These people often beg you to grant them special favors, give them cushy assignments, or ignore policies and rules because the whole world's against them. They always seem to be a day late, a dollar short, and victimized by circumstances beyond their control. They may break into tears or sigh and roll their eyes (like some adolescents you might know) when asked to do any task that involves a tight deadline or breaking a sweat.

Eager volunteers. If you think you can't have too many eager volunteers, think again. Like the Godfather, some of them have hidden agendas. After they've enthusiastically pitched in to

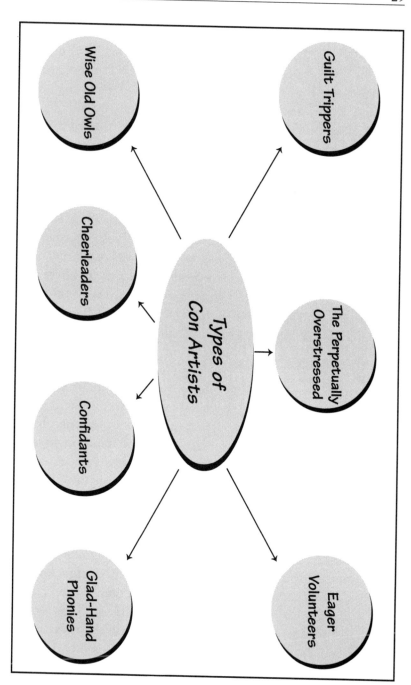

bail out troubled projects or serve on task forces, don't be surprised if they call in those markers by asking for special concessions. If you refuse, you'll find their volunteerism had a price tag. They expected you to bank their goodwill and repay it on demand. If you don't, they may turn hostile, obnoxious, or sullen because you didn't keep your part of their assumed bargain.

Wise old owls. These con artists have been around a long time, know the ropes with their eyes closed, and are happy to give their new boss (you) the benefit of their sage wisdom. But watch out. Wise old owls may be kissing up to you to enhance their own organizational clout. The implied power that comes from their connection with you can easily be abused, misrepresented, and used to gain leverage with their peers.

Cheerleaders. If you ask cheerleaders who's the greatest person of all, well, roll up your pants cuffs; things are gonna get a little deep. Cheerleaders lay on flattery by the ton. You're fantastic, perceptive, insightful, proactive, innovative, and always have your oil changed on time.

You're an all around jolly good fellow or gal, and they tell you so at every opportunity. Why? Because the more flattering cheerleaders are, the harder it will be for you to hurt their feelings by disagreeing with them, disciplining them, giving them a tough assignment, or telling them to stop messing around and start doing an honest day's work.

Best Tip
Don't be deceived by cheerleaders. Their incessant attempts to flatter are meant to keep your attention away from poor productivity.

I once had a cheerleader as a partner in a writing venture. We were supposed to critique each other's material, discuss possible changes, revise it, and send it on to the publisher.

My cheerleader partner was praise personified: "Your work's fabulous! I love it! Those words just jumped off the page! Man, how do you *do* it?" Meanwhile, I wasn't receiving any material from him—fabulous or otherwise. It soon became apparent that this guy wasn't willing to carry his share of the load but hoped he could con me into picking up most of it. No way. He was eventually dropped from the project, and a replacement came in to do his part.

Confidants. Confidants can lock up your secrets tighter than the gold in Fort Knox. And isn't that nice? You can speak freely and share your innermost problems and thoughts with them. They're your friends! But wait a minute . . . what if (perish the thought) you suddenly have a falling out?

Best **T**ip
Be careful when confiding your inmost thoughts to co-workers, but especially to subordinates. Your words may come back to bite you.

Well, watch your back. Confidants who become enemies know enough to ruin you.

Glad-hand phonies. These folks are cordial and fun to be around. They're always gripping and grinning, flattering (but not to excess), and generally being the life of the party. They love everybody—or so it seems.

But they show their true selves when people they dislike leave the room by making fun of them, spreading unflattering gossip, or otherwise ripping them up. It's hypocrisy's finest hour. And if your ears burn after *you* leave the room, well, don't be surprised.

Managing Con Artists

Seeing through con artists' gamesmanship is just half the issue. You also have to protect yourself against them without making them enemies, embarrassing them, calling their bluff, or otherwise revealing that you're onto them. How?

1. Delegate work as fairly as possible. Review your decisions to confirm that all who report to you, including con artists, receive their fair share of unpleasant assignments along with the plums. This is your best defense against employees who might otherwise accuse you of playing favorites, dumping on them, or giving in to con artists under pressure. Point out whenever the

opportunity arises that you're committed to balancing the work load evenly.

2. Don't let con artists monopolize your time. Giving them the lion's share of your attention implies to co-workers that they've got the inside track with you.

3. Be a stand-up manager. Say what you mean; mean what you say. Follow policies and procedures, because they exist to prevent arbitrary behavior. Realize that con artists who may have been able to manipulate your predecessor may badmouth your management style because it frustrates their own self-serving objectives.

Best Tip
Don't let procrastinators jeopardize deadlines and force snap decisions.

Don't negotiate assignments to pacify a con artist or let yourself be drawn into arrangements that would compromise your principles or ethics if the relationship turns sour. Workers respect managers who let them know exactly where they stand and don't play favorites.

4. Last but not least, try not to be too skeptical of people's motives. While it may be easy to interpret someone's words or actions as conniving or Machiavellian, there *are* lots of well-intentioned folks out there who mean their compliments sincerely, or honestly want to help. Some of them may work for you, and the more better. It would be an awful mistake to stereotype them as con artists.

THE PROCRASTINATOR

"Mañana is often the busiest day of the week."

SPANISH PROVERB

Procrastinators are close relatives of the wafflers you'll meet later in this chapter, but with at least one major difference. Wafflers flip-flop and reverse decisions, while procrastinators postpone or avoid them until time becomes critical. Then, when the crisis finally erupts, they may have to make a snap decision, which is usually little better than tossing a coin.

These folks are especially irritating to deal with when you're facing a deadline and need their input or support to meet it.

I had a boss in manufacturing who learned early in his career to put would-be procrastinators on notice. This habit, he confided, saved him lots of aggravation and frustration over the years.

"I don't like surprises," he always told new members of his staff. "I can deal with almost anything but that. The worst thing you can do if you work for me is hide emergencies, try to put out fires, or stew over department-wide problems that you haven't told me about and do nothing. If you do this and I get chewed out by higher management because you put off telling me, there'll be trouble. So get me in the boat with you, and we'll work together."

Managing Procrastinators

1. When you find that a procrastinator has put off a decision, request the person's help and ask some probing questions to uncover the true reason for the delay. For example:

- "What is it you need in the way of budget, personnel, equipment, or other resources that's holding you back on this decision?"
- "Who else is involved that may be hanging it up?"
- "Why are you reluctant to move forward with this?"

2. Apply discreet peer pressure. Describe the severity and cost of the problems this person has caused for other members of the team or group by sitting on the decision for so long. Knowing that he or she is seen as a bottleneck who's making life more complicated for co-workers may be enough incentive to make the procrastinator move off dead-center.

3. Emphasize the hazards of deciding by default. Procrastinators need to realize that no decision is, in itself, a decision. *Not* deciding means they've relinquished potential control over the matter and cast their fate to the winds.

4. Keep yourself approachable. One reason why procrastinators sometimes put off a decision or avoid informing the boss is because the boss has a tendency to shoot the messenger for bad news. So keep both your door and your mind open, and make every possible effort to get people to level with you when there's trouble, no matter how bad it might be.

Every time an employee summons the courage to bring you bad news, you have an opportunity to confirm that you're not going to blame the messenger for the message. A calm, unruffled reaction at these times is critical. Other people will take it as a model for how you'll behave toward them when it's their turn to bring you a damage report.

5. Set and agree on a deadline. If you're discussing an assignment with a suspected procrastinator, discuss this point very early in your conversation. Clarify the need for this person to deliver on time and the problems and ramifications if the work falls behind schedule. Get the procrastinator's unequivocal commitment with such remarks as:

- "Do you understand why I need the work delivered by this date?"
- "Can you think of any reason why you can't do the job on time? If so, we've got to discuss and resolve it now."
- "I'm asking for your firm promise to deliver this by the deadline. Do we understand each other?"

In addition, set up a series of checkpoints and milestones that will help the worker verify that he or she is both on track and on time. Confirm that you intend to follow up as often as necessary to monitor the person's progress and discuss whatever problems have come up before they turn into emergencies.

THE KNOW-IT-ALL

> *"Wisdom is not a product of schooling but of the*
> *lifelong attempt to acquire it."*
>
> Albert Einstein

These opinionated, outspoken folks have all the answers. Just ask them! Many of them are senior employees, hold highly specialized jobs, or have large egos. This isn't to say that know-it-alls have no value. On the contrary, some may be top-notch experts in their fields. The fact that they're not open to others' ideas and opinions, however, makes them irritating and counterproductive.

Know-it-alls relish an audience and the chance to show off their alleged expertise—factors you need to take into account when managing them.

Managing Know-It-Alls

1. Learn as much as possible about a situation or problem before you discuss it with a know-it-all. That way you can anticipate and defuse some of the know-it-all's authoritative comments and keep from sounding like the green kid who's learning at the master's knee.

2. Avoid yielding the floor to know-it-alls during meetings. When you ask their opinion, you invite them to monopolize the discussion. It's the quickest way to lose control. If you want their input on an issue, ask for it privately so they won't be sounding off in front of a large audience.

Best Tip

Don't discount the value of a know-it-all's opinions. Just keep them in perspective.

3. Flatter them tactfully. Know-it-alls respond well to judicious ego-stroking, and if done sparingly, it makes them predisposed to like you. Going overboard with praise, however, gives them the impression that you're overly impressed with them—which only makes them harder to manage.

4. Don't reject the know-it-all's input. It may really be valuable. Instead, tactfully add your own suggestions to the know-it-all's ideas. ("That sounds like a good technique, Paul. How do you think it might work in the other two departments? If we tried it there, we'd have more feedback to base our decision on. What do you think?")

5. Refuse to play the role of student. When I was first starting out in management, I had a pompous know-it-all in my
work group whose favorite opening line was, "Lesson Number
One: . . ." after which he'd deliver a long-winded lecture on the
issue. This irritated the daylights out of me.

The second time he launched into a discourse, I raised both
hands to chest-height, mustered a smile, and said, "Hold on a
minute. I respect your experience, but I want you to share it a
little differently. I'm not comfortable with this 'lesson' business.
Just tell me what's on your mind, OK?" After I repeated this line
on three or four occasions, the guy got the message and stopped
coming on like Father Knows Best.

6. Use the know-it-all as a mentor. True, you don't want to
look subservient or worshipful. But then again, a know-it-all who
is an acknowledged expert can give you insights born of many
years of experience—and give your job knowledge and career a
major boost into the bargain.

So listen courteously, question carefully, and acknowledge an ex-
pert know-it-all's know-how. As a mentor, he or she may save you lots of wasted time, false starts,
and avoidable mistakes. Such a relationship can be priceless dur-
ing the foundation years of your career.

Best Tip
Keep the know-it-all off bal-ance by refusing to play the role of student. You'll only encourage more condescend-ing behavior.

THE CLAM

"Let your questions focus on the other person. Say, 'What do
you think?' rather than 'Do you agree with me?'"

BARRY FARBER, RADIO INTERVIEWER, IN *MAKING PEOPLE TALK*

Clams give off no verbal or body-language clues to what they
really think. They're about as expressive as a zombie holding
four aces. Clams remind me of Yul Brynner's robot gunfighter in

the classic futuristic film *Westworld*—cold-eyed, impassive, and thoroughly noncommittal. But with any luck, the clams you'll meet at work won't be as heavily armed.

One of my most exasperating workplace clams was a fellow we called "Mumbles." He was an introverted retired military colonel who made little eye contact with anyone and spoke in a monotone—while looking at the top of his desk or his shoes. Ask him to clarify what he said, and he'd only mumble louder.

Best Tip

Do your best to open up clams. They often harbor some tasty morsels of insight and innovation.

This clam's communication skills were so bad that some of us would ask our co-workers to sit in on meetings to help us decipher Mumbles's mumblings afterward. Perhaps he had a psychological problem; we never knew. But Mumbles was a clam's clam.

A clam's tendency to shut people out is both disconcerting ("What's she *really* thinking?") and harmful to progress ("What ideas is he holding back that might help us solve this problem?")

Managing Clams

1. Perhaps the best way to pry open clams is by asking open-ended questions that force them to expand on their feelings. Asking them yes-or-no questions will produce the predictable response—cryptic monosyllable comments or a noncommittal shrug. So try questions such as:

- "Tell me what you think about . . ."
- "When should we . . ."
- "Why do you believe . . ."
- "How could we . . ."
- "Tell me more about . . ."
- "Describe how we should . . ."

2. Identify the claim's major skills, talents, and interests. Re-

ferring to these may be one way to get him or her to show some signs of life. ("Roger, I know you're really into home improvement. Let's imagine this assignment is one of those remodeling projects I've heard you like to do. How would you organize it and map out an action plan?")

3. Don't go overboard trying to elicit enthusiasm from clams who work for you, especially if they're doing a good job. Some folks prefer to be left alone. Moreover, those who are dyed-in-the-wool introverts may feel harassed or embarrassed by too much cajoling or attention and may even resign as a result.

THE WAFFLER

"Indecision and delays are the parents of failure."

GEORGE CANNING

With wafflers, no decision is ever final. They may make a decision this morning and rescind or modify it this afternoon. They have second thoughts. And third ones. And perhaps a few more after that. They reverse themselves more often than a bulldozer and move backwards more often than a lobster. They're the organizational version of perpetual bachelors—afraid to make a firm commitment and stand behind it.

What's so exasperating about wafflers is that you can't really be sure that their word is final. This is especially irritating if you have a waffling boss and you can't act without his or her approval. Waffling bosses may authorize you to do something today, then reconsider it tomorrow.

Waffling employees may create problems too, because they can rethink and stew over an issue without making a lick of progress. And they can sit on problems or opportunities until things reach critical mass. Welcome to Malfunction Junction.

Managing Wafflers

1. If the waffler is your boss, try to nail down his or her instructions or decision by asking for written confirmation ("Can

I have a memo for my files just in case?"). But take things one step further: write the memo for the waffler's signature (which may prevent waffling on the commitment not to waffle).

2. If your waffler is a subordinate, some training in decision making may be in order. The employee may have trouble clearly defining the problem or opportunity, clarifying alternatives, gathering information on each one, or dealing with other key steps in the decision-making process (see *The Agile Manager's Guide to Making Effective Decisions*).

3. Give subordinate wafflers a deadline for the decision. Let them know that you require a firm position so you can plan accordingly and commit the necessary resources. A Waffler's indecision can't be allowed to threaten your team's or department's success.

4. If the waffler reports to you, make sure he or she understands which of you will fill out the waffler's performance evaluation! Wafflers who impair the perfor-

Best Tip

Don't allow wafflers to delay a decision until time becomes critical.

mance of your department or work group must be held accountable for their actions. And while this isn't to suggest that you be threatening or vindictive, the employee's tendency to waffle may make the difference between an acceptable and an outstanding rating—and its corresponding pay increase. A little honesty here can go a long way.

5. Clarify the potential consequences if the waffler won't commit—that is, the fact that waffling on decision *A* may have a domino effect on related decisions *B*, *C*, and *D*, and what this chain reaction may cost the company in lost time or missed opportunities. Wafflers must know that their irksome behavior may cause trouble that could be laid on their doorstep.

6. Depending on the circumstances, you might take a waffling boss's first decision and run with it. Later, if he or she decides to reverse course, you can point out that you've com-

mitted resources based on your boss's original position, things have now passed the point of no return, and you can't back out without causing massive problems. (This is a variation of the maxim, "It's easier to beg forgiveness than ask permission.") You shouldn't be blamed for acting on the waffler's word if there were no conditions attached.

THE JOLLY JOKER

"[Abrasive people] must be told very early on how their behavior undermines them. All too often afraid to do this, their bosses quickly become resentful and withdraw, leaving their subordinates uncomfortable but not knowing why. Feeling anxious, the abrasive subordinate then attempts to win back the regard and esteem of the boss in the only way he knows, by intensifying this behavior. That only makes things worse."

Harry Levinson, Psychologist, Harvard Medical School

Jolly jokers are the type to hide a Whoopee Cushion on the CEO's chair or put plastic vomit in front of the water fountain. And while some levity can be refreshing in an uptight, button-down corporate culture, people who cross the line too often or too far can be distracting and, well, irritating.

Moreover, some jolly jokers may employ barbed humor to harpoon or belittle their co-workers and members of management (including you). If you protest, they may act hurt, claim it's "all in good fun," complain that you "can't take a joke," or tell you to "lighten up" or "chill out." Your objections make you look like a sorehead or a curmudgeon, because everybody's supposed to love a clown, right?

The trouble is, a jolly joker's steady barrage of unrestrained or ill-timed humor can derail a team's train of thought, diminish the gravity or importance of a critical meeting or major decision, or simply keep pounding away at something like a dog gnawing a bone, to a point where it ruins a once-pleasant relationship.

I had a pal for some ten years who was a Renaissance man. I considered him my best friend. We spent hours talking about everything, including cars, favorite books and authors, target shooting, lawn care, and the ambiance of various Central Florida pubs.

But somewhere along the line, he started needling me about being an enthusiastic booster of my alma mater's football team. Every time we got together, he'd crank up a barrage of wisecracks and snide remarks. I told him several times that his humor was starting to get irritating and his jokes were wearing thin. I got tired of hearing the same old lines, week after week.

Like all jolly jokers, he swore it was all in fun, but that didn't make him any less irritating. Eventually I stopped hanging out with him altogether. I still miss his overall camaraderie, but it just wasn't worth the hassle.

Jolly jokers can also be hazardous to themselves and others, especially if they're carrying fire-

Best Tip

Keep a lid on jolly jokers. They can derail team effort— and morale—awfully fast.

arms. One jolly joker sheriff's lieutenant in Orlando, Florida, reportedly:

- Jumped out of the dark and frightened a rookie deputy on her first stakeout.
- Threw a rubber snake to scare colleagues, visitors, and children.
- Told offensive jokes.
- Pulled a chair out from under a fellow deputy—twice.

Despite outstanding performance evaluations, his offbeat sense of humor led to his demotion to sergeant. Humor, like beauty, is sometimes in the eye of the beholder.

Managing Jolly Jokers

1. Don't debate them. Debating can easily lead into a no-win "That's not funny"/"Aw, you can't take a joke" exchange that resolves nothing.

Rather than arguing about whose opinion is valid, stick to the facts: The joker's behavior is disrupting the work, irritating co-workers, creating unnecessary friction, or making others feel uncomfortable. And it's your feelings and theirs—not the joker's— that must be respected and acknowledged.

2. Lay it on the line. Tell the prankster in no uncertain terms what situations or subjects are off-limits. Ill-considered wisecracks with racial or sexual overtones, for example, could cause your company to be hit with an expensive lawsuit—which is no laughing matter. So-called practical jokes may cause injury and lead to a worker's compensation claim.

3. Lead by example. Set the workplace tone that you expect from your people (which doesn't have to be dry and humorless—merely professional). Don't compromise yourself by seeming to go along with the joker's inappropriate humor or pranks just to stay on his or her good side. This gives tacit approval to the disruptive behavior.

THE WORRYWART

> *"Worry is interest you pay on a debt that may never come due."*
>
> ANONYMOUS

Worrywarts are in their glory when there's a potential crisis. They may need heavy intravenous doses of Maalox and Xanax. Look up "anxiety" in the dictionary, and you'll find a worrywart's picture. Like Chicken Little or the perpetually hyper Aunt Pittypat in *Gone With the Wind*, they're prone to screech, preach, and beseech about the awful catastrophe they're sure is going happen. Often, it doesn't.

Left unmanaged, worrywarts can spread panic like an epidemic among their more impressionable co-workers. And if there really *is* a crisis, the last thing people need to do is panic. So you need to shut worrywarts up—or at least calm them down.

Managing Worrywarts

1. Consider screening worrywarts out of the communications loop if there's bad news they don't need to know about. What they don't know won't hurt them. More important, it won't set off their internal alarm and cause them to get everybody else all stirred up. This is especially important if there's an unfounded rumor floating around that needs to be discouraged. The longer you can keep it away from the worrywart, the better off everyone will be.

2. Ignore their doomsaying and hysterics as much as possible. Your behavior could be contagious in a positive way. The fact that you're playing it cool may, in fact, have a calming effect on them.

3. If possible, put a positive spin on bad news you must deliver to worrywarts. Since they're quick to pick up on negative feelings and go charging off in all directions, try to show them that the glass is half full instead of half empty.

Best Tip

Watch worrywarts closely. Left unmanaged, they can cause mass panic among your work group.

THE NAYSAYER

"Fire the doubters out of your life."

Ray Bradbury

Optimism isn't in a naysayer's dictionary. These folks are negative about practically everything. If it's sunny, they'll point out that there's no rain. If it's raining, they'll note that there's no sunshine.

The worst naysayers are those who love to throw a monkey wrench into the works just to see what'll happen, or mindlessly rattle off negative comments that can be distressing if not downright harmful. When Bob, a colleague of mine, returned to work after triple bypass heart surgery, most of us congratulated him on how great he looked and how much better he was going to feel.

The naysayer in our group, however, informed him in some detail that bypasses didn't always work out and that he might have to have his redone within a five years or so. But hey, Bob, have a nice day anyway!

Naysayers are often technical or scientific types who are steeped in logic and groomed to deal with facts and hard information. Their preoccupation with details, documentation, and data can disrupt a team's harmony and derail its creative train of thought.

When it comes to brainstorming, naysayers can be especially toxic. Their negativism can kill creativity deader than last Thanksgiving's turkey. Unless they're kept on a tight leash (or excluded), you can count on naysayers to ignore the roses and point out the thorns every time.

Managing Naysayers

1. Because naysayers often get bogged down with details (ask them what time it is and they'll tell you how their watch was made), don't let them hold you a verbal hostage. If you need a naysayer's input on something, try steering the conversation with comments such as:

- "Give me your one-minute summary of . . ." (I can't afford to get wrapped up in a ten-minute discussion.)
- "Let's skip the details for now." (I only want the big-picture view.)
- "Let's get past these fine points and deal with the larger issue of . . ." (The details aren't important; they may not even be your concern.)

- "I'm going to let you go now." (I've got work to do. I can't listen to you rattle on any longer.)
- "I've got an appointment in 10 minutes, but we can talk until then." (That's all the time I can afford to spend with you.)

2. Ignore or disregard the naysayer's gloomy comments whenever possible. Acknowledging them implies that you're impressed and only encourages more of the same.

3. Take the wind out of naysayers' sails and neutralize their impact by briefly acknowledging the issue's negatives before they do. That prevents them from catching you off guard or grabbing the spotlight and upstaging you. ("We're all aware of this plan's potential drawbacks. There's no point in going over them again. What we need to look at in this meeting are its potential benefits.")

4. Use naysayers as resources whenever possible. By their very nature, they're the perfect devil's advocate. If they can find a flaw in your argument, they will. When you're coming down to the wire on a decision and have moved beyond the creative thinking stage, naysayers can give it a final reality check.

Best Tip

Be careful how you use naysayers—they are often technical or scientific people who have difficulty "thinking outside the box."

5. Use role-reversal to turn a naysayer into a "yea" sayer. This tactic may succeed because of the naysayer's tendency to disagree with whatever you say no matter what. Sometimes the more you insist that an idea won't work, the harder the naysayer works to show you that it will.

I knew one manager who became very adept at manipulating her naysaying boss by taking a negative position from the start—and allowing him to talk her out of it. Their conversations typically went like this:

"I've got an idea . . . I doubt that it'll work, but what the heck. I thought I'd bounce it off you anyhow."

"Won't work? How do you know it won't work if you haven't tried it?"

"Well, I'm skeptical. It just seems like . . ."

"Don't be so hasty. Sit down and let's talk about it."

"Well, okay, if you insist. What might happen if we . . . "

Bingo!

6. Throw down a challenge. Pressure the naysayer to produce solutions, not just criticisms. For example: "Jack, you're a great devil's advocate, but how about applying that talent in a different direction. How do you suggest we deal with this situation?" "Ellen, we agree that this proposal has a downside. Let's move past that and talk about how we can make it work. Give me your ideas."

At worst, this practice may cause the naysayer to knock off the negativism. At best, he or she may produce some suggestions that nobody else has thought of yet.

THE GENETIC JERK

"[Office] politics is the process of getting along with the querulous, the garrulous and the congenitally unlovable."

MARILYN MOATS KENNEDY, PARTNER, CAREER STRATEGIES, INC.

Ever see a bumper sticker that says, "Places to go, people to annoy"? Well when you do, look at who's behind the wheel. Unless it's a borrowed car, odds are the driver's a genetic jerk. Irritating is the genetic jerk's middle name. These folks get off on being obnoxious just for the hell of it; they don't really care what they say, how, where, or to whom.

If you work with such folks, take comfort in the likelihood that they'll likely meet their Waterloo someday. Hey, if it happened to Napoleon, it can happen to them. At least you can hope so! And when their payback comes, whether it's from co-workers, family members, or the guy in the car they just cut off in traffic, the results can be pretty nasty.

According to sports writers, television commentators, and even numerous alumni, fans, and boosters, University of Florida football coach Steve Spurrier reportedly fits the description of a genetic jerk to a T. Strong record and coaching acumen notwithstanding, "Coach Superior," as he's called by some sports writers, has an abrasive, belligerent personality that has made him one of college football's least popular coaches.

Best Tip

Avoid genetic jerks. They have an inborn tendency to be aggravating.

He contracts foot-in-mouth disease several times each season, which has alienated some of the very people and groups whose good will more savvy coaches seek to cultivate. At various times he has:

- Fired off acrimonious faxes to sports columnists who have criticized his coaching strategy.
- Physically confronted prominent television sportscaster Keith Jackson months after Jackson suggested he may have run up the score in a lopsided victory over a no-name opponent.
- Criticized his own players to the news media in post-game press conferences.
- Declared that his team played "like a bunch of losers" after an especially stinging defeat to a major rival.

Managing Genetic Jerks

Frankly, genetic jerks are about as unmanageable as they are abominable. Your options for dealing with them, unlike most other types of irritating people, are pretty limited. But here goes.

1. If your boss or some of your peers are genetic jerks, perhaps your best course is to avoid them whenever possible. When

you can't avoid them, at least try to keep them at arm's length. Communicate with them indirectly, whether by e-mail, fax, interoffice memo, or carrier pigeon. The less you have to see them face to face, the lower your blood pressure will be.

2. If the genetic jerks work for you, the outlook is somewhat better.

- Do everything possible to transfer them to another department or position where you won't have to work with them anymore. You need to rid yourself of their aggravation. (Note: Remember that dumping your problems on another manager won't endear you to them or improve your reputation. At the least, let people know what's coming.)

- If you can't get rid of them, at least try to physically move them to some remote location outside your normal traffic pattern. If your company has a corporate Siberia, pack their bags and send them off. Sayonara. Bon Voyage. And please *don't* keep in touch.

- If their irritating behavior has a negative impact on their job performance, and you've warned them repeatedly about the need to overhaul their conduct, have no regrets about downsizing them at the first opportunity. And if this sounds a bit callous, just turn back a page or two and review their miserable behavior traits once again. No organization needs people who perpetually disrupt their co-workers' peace of mind and productivity day in and day out.

THE PSYCHOTIC

"A problem worker is usually a worker with a problem."

SAMUEL B. KUTASH, RUTGERS U., IN LEADERSHIP IN THE OFFICE

While thousands of managers probably agree with Kutash's quotation, they're equally likely to agree that so-called problem workers cause problems for everyone in their workplace. Psychotic problem workers, like genetic jerks, can be some of the most irritating people of all.

You may have heard the wisecrack that neurotics build castles in the air, psychotics live in them, and their psychiatrists collect the rent. But dealing with someone who is genuinely deranged is no laughing matter.

Moreover, the Americans with Disabilities Act protects both mentally and physically ill employees, so agile managers must proceed carefully when working with employees who may suffer from mental disabilities. According to the EEOC, complaints of discrimination based on mental illness amounted to 16 percent of all complaints filed in 1998 and made up the largest single category of all.

I spoke with a manager recently who's had to deal with a psychotic employee, and hers is not a happy experience. "I've always been the kind of person who was slow to anger," she said, "but 'Alice' has really found a way to push my buttons. I've spent hours trying to figure out what I might have said or done to make her behave like she does, and I just don't know."

Best Tip

Handle psychotics with care. They may be out of touch with reality.

This worker has filed numerous EEOC complaints—all cleared after an investigation—alleging this supervisor was prejudiced against her because of her national origin.

Moreover, "Alice" seems convinced that this manager is somehow responsible for everything bad that's ever happened to her. She's apparently dedicated to making this boss's life miserable through a combination of unfounded formal grievances and subtle behind-the-scenes rumor mongering and vicious, ill-concealed character assassination.

The manager suspects that, given "Alice's" poor English skills, she may have misinterpreted a remark or failed to grasp a nuance in one of their long-ago conversations and took offense where none existed.

Regardless of what may have caused the conflict, each conversation usually starts on a hostile note and ends with acrimonious accusations and threats of additional EEOC complaints for alleged discrimination.

Coping with Psychotics

Note the change in wording for the above heading compared to the other ones in this guide. There's a good reason. Although you can hope to "manage" other types of irritating people, "coping" may be the best you can do with psychotics.

1. Consider using a subordinate as a buffer when dealing with the psychotic employee. This in no way suggests that you hide behind this delegate or make him or her a scapegoat or target for the psychotic's erratic behavior. But if you can identify a co-worker who is able to communicate successfully with the problem employee, he or she may be the best person to relay information and give instructions.

2. Keep a paper trail of your conversations with the troubled employee. Note dates, times, locations, the topic of your discussions, and specific remarks the person made. You may have to terminate a psychotic for the benefit and safety of your department if he or she is disruptive, hostile, threatening, or behaving erratically. In such cases, you'll need to prepare a solid defense against a likely EEOC complaint.

3. Avoid confrontations and arguments whenever possible. You'll gain little or nothing and may only cause the person's hostility to escalate.

The Agile Manager's Checklist

Con Artists
✔ Delegate work fairly to everyone.
✔ Don't let them monopolize your time.
✔ Say what you mean and mean what you say.

Procrastinators
✔ Find out what's causing the delay.
✔ Emphasize the hazards of deciding by default.
✔ Set and agree on a clear deadline for the decision.
✔ Establish checkpoints to help them stay on schedule.

Know-It-Alls
✔ Understand the situation before involving them.
✔ Try not to ask their opinion in meetings.
✔ Flatter them tactfully; they'll tend to like you for it.
✔ Try combining your ideas with theirs to get them to consider your viewpoint.

Clams
✔ Ask open-ended questions that force them to answer with more than "yes" or "no."
✔ Don't overdo it. Excessive attention can make clams feel embarrassed or harassed.

Wafflers
✔ If the waffler is your boss, request written confirmation of the instructions or decision.
✔ Give subordinate wafflers training in how to make effective decisions.
✔ Give wafflers a deadline for the decision and stick to it.

Jolly Jokers
✔ Don't debate them; emphasize the negative consequences of their alleged humor.
✔ Spell out situations and subjects that are off-limits to their humor regardless of their intent.
✔ Lead by example. Be serious if you expect them to be.

Worrywarts
✔ Tell them no more bad news than is absolutely necessary.
✔ Ignore their doomsaying and hysterics.
✔ Deliver bad news with a positive spin.

Naysayers
✔ Disregard their negative comments whenever possible.
✔ Use them as devil's advocates.
✔ Challenge naysayers to produce solutions, not criticism.

Checklist, continued

Genetic Jerks

✔ If they're your boss or co-workers, avoid them whenever possible.

✔ If they report to you, try to transfer them elsewhere, move them to a remote location, or downsize them out of your life as soon as possible.

Psychotics

✔ Deal with them through a subordinate or some other intermediary if possible.

✔ Keep a detailed record of your volatile discussions to justify a termination should that become necessary.

✔ Avoid confrontations and arguments. That may make a psychotic even more hostile.

Chapter Three

Types of Irritating People: Relationships

"No one can drive you crazy unless you give them the keys."

ANONYMOUS

"You bring a great number of skills to the table, Phil. I'm glad that industry committee finally recognized your abilities by giving you an award. You deserved it."

Phil beamed, and his eyes seemed to grow larger behind his soda-bottle-bottom glasses.

"I can't say I'm exactly happy with how the team has handled this new project, though."

Phil stopped smiling. He leaned forward and said, "The team has some members with what I'd call less than stellar credentials. I was hoping you'd put me on the other project with Will, Tony, and the others—not this one. Some of my so-called teammates need remedial help. Just the other day, Janet—"

"Phil," interrupted the Agile Manager. "I have complete confidence in the people on this project, including you. Everyone has precisely the skills needed to pull this off. Did you know Janet worked on the 750C for Murphy Technology? Hers was a key role."

Phil's face dropped at the mention of that legendary product. "She did? She never told me that. I would have given her more respect, I mean, um . . ."

"And Bobby, though young, graduated from Cal Tech in two and half years. He's come up with a couple of innovations I think are brilliant."

The Agile Manager paused, then continued: "Now Phil, you have a lot to add to the team. When you denigrate others—especially behind their backs—you demotivate them. Two people asked to be taken off the project, and they both mentioned you as the reason. One of them said you constantly second guess his work, and the other said you point out negatives all day long. Is this true?"

"Well," said Phil slowly, "from my point of view all I'm doing is telling the truth. And if I see a better way of doing something, it's hard for me to keep my mouth shut."

"Your 'better way' of pursuing this project cost us a week, and I can't have that," said the Agile Manager, the tension in his voice rising. Keep cool, he said to himself. Keep cool.

Phil seemed to look inward with a quizzical look on his face. Nobody had questioned his performance since he won the award. "Well," he said even more slowly than before, "I . . ." He never finished the sentence.

The Agile Manager said, "Can you keep your thoughts to yourself until this project is done? If you really disagree with the way we're pursuing it, you can talk to me or Anita. And cut the sniping, OK? If you're really not happy in this department, maybe I can find another spot for you."

"No!" said Phil. "No . . . I don't want to go anywhere else."

Some irritating behavior may be more work-based than personality-based, although I'll be the first to agree that the subject's debatable. Anyway, let's check out people here whose aggravating conduct may surface mostly on the job but doesn't necessarily spill over to their lives after they lock up their desks and head off to celebrate happy hour at the Prancing Aardvark pub down the street.

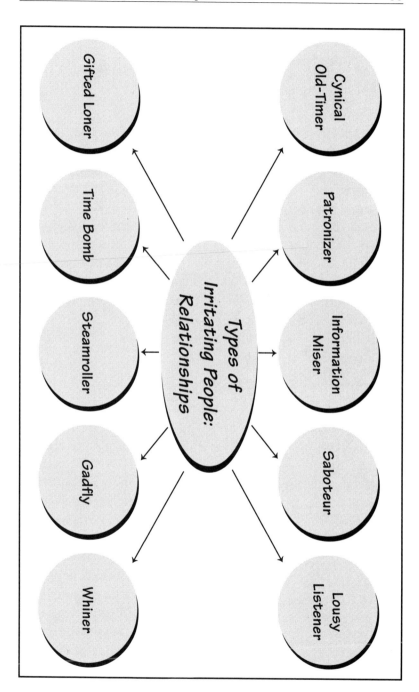

Types of
Irritating People:
Relationships

Gifted Loner

Cynical
Old-Timer

Time Bomb

Patronizer

Steamroller

Information
Miser

Gadfly

Saboteur

Whiner

Lousy
Listener

THE CYNICAL OLD-TIMER

"Cynic: One who not only reads bitter lessons from the past, but who is prematurely disappointed with the future."

ANONYMOUS

Cynical old-timers have been there, done that, and seen it all—as they love to point out again and again. One of my former co-workers used to recite the line "During my twenty-five years of business and industry experience . . ." so often that the rest of us wanted to set it to music. And yes, we saw evidence that he only had about five years of experience repeated five times over.

Cynical old-timers poison the well of enthusiasm for everybody else. Their negativism dulls the edge of excitement for eager new hires, throws a wet blanket over hot proposals, and kills potentially innovative ideas at birth. They shake their heads or chuckle patronizingly when anybody makes an optimistic comment. Look up "grinch" in the dictionary, and you'll likely find a picture of one of them.

Managing Cynical Old-Timers

1. Try to channel their cynicism in a positive direction by listening to their reminiscences. This won't cost you a dime. If you're a newcomer, these old war horses can sometimes be terrific resources.

They're a mother lode of insights into how your corporate culture evolved, where some of the bodies are buried, who the major movers and shakers are, and why business is done as it is. When viewed and managed positively, they're walking timelines of your organization's history.

Best Tip

Tap into the experience cynical old-timers have. Just do your best to hold their cynicism at bay.

2. Recruit them as allies. Acknowledge the value of their experience and point out their leadership potential by virtue of

the fact that people may look up to them as old pros. Daimler-Chrysler recognized the value of retired production line employees when management decided to resume making convertibles a few years ago.

Practically no existing employees knew the key assembly techniques and tricks of the trade that were used to build convertibles in the 1950s and 1960s. Consequently, management recruited many retired old-timers who had built convertibles during their heyday to return to work as consultants and trainers on the new convertible production line.

Best Tip

Channel the cynicism of the old-timers by listening to their reminiscences. Sometimes they'll tell you where the bodies are buried.

3. Get close to them. You can't change their behavior from a distance. If you're supervising them, try to develop a close working relationship by involving them in key projects or major decisions where their experience—if separated from their cynicism—can be an asset. Even the most sour apples can be sweetened over time.

4. Do your homework before engaging them in debate. Cynical old-timers like to catch the "youngsters" off guard or make them look naïve. If you study up on an issue, you might be able to deflate their obnoxious, blustering cynicism diplomatically with a concise comment or question. For example:

- "The reason why we didn't try that five years ago was because we didn't have the budget. Now we do."
- "This idea has been a money-maker for X percent of our competitors. If they can make it work, why can't we?"
- "The top management team back then didn't provide enough support. Our new one will."
- "Most of us are convinced that this is the right way to go, and we've made a commitment. We really don't want to leave you behind."

5. Make a direct appeal for support: "I need your involve-

ment to make this program succeed, Bob. The rest of the group looks up to you; they'll follow your lead. Will you work with me on this?"

Without being Pollyanna or a happy, peppy puppy, maintain a positive, upbeat outlook. Agile Managers know this comes with the territory. Try to smother cynicism with enthusiasm. This tactic may eventually wear down (or at least discourage) the old-timer's jaundiced point of view. Enthusiasm can be as contagious as negativism. Hang in there, and keep your chin up.

THE PATRONIZER

"Nothing in the world is more haughty than a [person] of moderate capacity when once raised to power."

BARON WESSENBERG

Patronizers act condescending with most people—including their bosses—to inflate their own sense of importance. They often put down or discount colleagues' ideas. Many are also consciously or unconsciously sexist. Their behavior is tantamount to patting you on the head like a good little girl or boy.

One of the more memorable patronizers I've known habitually referred to females as "little lady" or "sweetheart" and people with less seniority as "junior" or "youngster." He also had the habit of placing his hand on your shoulder when he talked. His height (6'2"), coupled with his demeaning nicknames, made the gesture especially irritating. He was literally "talking down" to most people.

Managing Patronizers

Some patronizers don't have a clue that they're being offensive. Others conveniently ignore it. Perhaps the best way to manage them is to confront their behavior head-on (or, in the words of a good-ol'-boy pal of mine, "When you see trouble coming, go down the road to meet it."). And while you should try to make your point without making an enemy, you'll probably have to tell a condescending patronizer that enough is enough. Subtle suggestions tend to go right over their heads.

The patronizing colleague I mentioned above got his come-uppance when a female manager took over our department. After he called her "little lady" a couple of times during their first lengthy meeting, she quietly closed the door and said, "I resent being talked to that way, and

Confront patronizers directly when they try to inflate their own importance by putting others down.

I want to make that very clear to you. It's condescending; I think you know that. I look forward to our working together for a long time, but from here on, use my first name, or no name, but knock off the 'little lady' business."

This professionally delivered ultimatum made the fellow's jaw drop momentarily (he later admitted), but he reevaluated his behavior—as well as the fact that she was his boss—and chose his words more carefully from that day on. The "juniors" and "youngsters" could have taken an equally assertive position.

THE INFORMATION MISER

"Working with people is difficult, but not impossible."

GRAFFITI ON COPYING MACHINE, GEORGE WASHINGTON U.

Information is power, and information misers are intoxicated with it. While they're often found in information systems or computer services jobs, they can really be lurking at any cross-roads on your company's information highway, hiding in the underbrush, ready to ambush any information that might pass by and hold it for ransom—or just for the hell of it.

They're control freaks. Like millionaire John D. Rockefeller, who handed out shiny dimes to small children, information misers dole out their hoard of information sparingly and may expect much groveling as they do.

A number of years ago I ran into a pair of information misers on the faculty at one academic institution. Each actually did the work of two men (Laurel and Hardy), but that's beside the point. These guys stumbled across some information about a new doctoral program that didn't have a residency requirement. They promptly clamped a lid on it while they maneuvered to set themselves up as the contact people their colleagues would have to go through to apply for the program.

> **Best Tip**
>
> Don't let information misers clog up your organization. It thrives on timely information that must flow freely.

When the rest of us heard about it from another source, our first thought was, "Why should we bother dealing with these guys? They don't even work for that university!" The answer was, we shouldn't. They were only trying to inflate their own importance by stonewalling preliminary information on the program's status and development.

Information misers can frustrate clear communications, form logjams, pour sand in the gears of progress, and create unnecessary work and aggravation for everyone who wants or needs whatever data they're guarding so jealously.

Managing Information Misers

1. Information misers may move only if prodded. Using an electric cattle prod may sound like a good idea, but somebody's likely to overhear their screams. Moreover, it might short-circuit their pacemakers. So first try prodding them with a memo. At least you've started a paper trail in case you get the runaround and have to take more drastic measures.

Spell out what data you need, in what format, and when. Don't bother justifying your request unless the miser is your superior. To do so would make you appear subservient. The simple fact that you need it to do your job and the miser has control of it should be enough.

2. Make a note of any roadblocks, lame excuses, delays, or other irritations that the miser throws in your path. This information can be used later to help you identify and cope with the miser's typical response patterns. Agile managers anticipate and prepare for such hassles in advance.

3. Get your name on the miser's distribution list for essential information. Again, it's none of the miser's business why you want it. As long as you need it to do your job (and the data falls within your security classification, if confidential) nothing else should matter.

4. Ask for your boss's support. This may be necessary if the miser is at or above your boss's level and keeps stonewalling you despite your written request.

5. If you're forced to use certain information in critical correspondence and you believe it's not current, make that point and summarize your attempts to update it. Recipients should know that it's the information miser's fault, not yours, that the material may be dated. Don't be the fall guy. If a problem arises because the miser played delaying tactics or refused to cooperate, use the notes you kept above to defend yourself and expose the miser's irritating behavior to higher management.

THE SABOTEUR

> *"May the forces of evil become confused*
> *on the way to your house."*
>
> GEORGE CARLIN

Saboteurs may be driven by a number of motives: jealousy, insecurity, revenge, and resentment, to name a few. Those who are after your job will go to great lengths to discredit you or undermine your authority.

Saboteurs act a lot like the villains in James Bond movies, but without the benefit of high-tech weapons or a tank of piranhas (thank goodness). It's hard to catch them in the open; by definition they prefer stealth and sneak attacks. Their most popular weapons include lying, telling half-truths, criticizing you behind your back, spreading rumors, and damning with faint praise, all of which may be used to turn your boss and subordinates against you and/or assassinate your character.

Managing Saboteurs

1. Publicize your achievements. Make sure your boss, peers, and other appropriate parties realize how good you are. Outstanding performance is the best defense against a saboteur's sniping and rumor-mongering.

2. Follow the Godfather's advice: Keep your friends close and your enemies closer. Although you may have to grit your teeth and count to ten, maintain a close and cordial working relationship with the saboteur. Why? Because he or she will look all the more hypocritical for bad-mouthing you when your back's turned.

3. Radiate self-confidence. As the deodorant slogan goes, "Never let them see you sweat." Showing signs that the saboteur's tactics are affecting your work or temperament may be interpreted as weakness and may lend credibility to any lies or half-truths that the saboteur has spread. So remain captain of your own fate, maintain your course and speed, and keep things on an even keel.

Watch your back. Saboteurs prefer stealth and sneak attacks.

4. Put your opinions and position on key issues in writing. This minimizes a saboteur's ability to twist your words, take them out of context, or interpret them in ways you never intended.

5. Mentally edit and censor your remarks when you're in a saboteur's presence. Don't speak candidly or take such a person into your confidence. That would be a fatal mistake, no matter how closely you work together or what problems or projects you're collaborating on right now.

6. Keep your behavior above reproach. Any lapse of conduct could play right into a saboteur's hands. For example, one executive attended a conference with a highly subversive employee. When they went out to dinner together, the executive lowered his guard and got bombed on margaritas. He was stopped and charged with driving while intoxicated on their way back to the hotel. But hey, not to worry! The saboteur's uncle was the county sheriff!

You can guess the rest. He convinced his uncle to cover up the whole thing, and from that day on he had his boss right in his pocket. A major promotion followed some months later. (Thanks, boss. You really know how to return a favor!)

7. Consider confrontation. You can't allow a sniper's tactics to undermine your personal effectiveness and your department's performance. Consequently, you may have to call the saboteur out and say in so many words, "This can't continue. You've got to knock it off."

> **Best Tip**
>
> Understand that sometimes you'll have to confront saboteurs. You'll gain respect when you do.

I knew a very intense, slightly built supervisor who did just that. For whatever reasons, one of his employees started calling him "The Little Executive" and "That idiot in the corner office" when he wasn't around. The rest of the group picked up on these derogatory references, which jeopardized the supervisor's authority.

Finally, he decided it was time for a showdown. He called the employee in and calmly said, "I know about the stuff you're calling me behind my back. I want you to tell me why you're doing it." The worker had no sound reason, of course. All he could do was mumble something to the effect that he "wasn't really serious."

"Well, I'm taking it seriously," said the supervisor, "and I'm a big enough person to look you in the eye and say so. What you think of me personally doesn't matter. I wouldn't bother trying to change your opinion. But I called you in to tell you that your behavior's got to change for the sake of this group's productivity and morale. I won't allow either of them to be undermined. I'm giving you one of three choices: apply for a transfer to another department, turn in your resignation, or knock this garbage off, starting from the time you leave my office. Now, which is it going to be?"

The guy took the third option.

When word of their frank discussion circulated through the grapevine, other members of the group respected the boss for confronting the saboteur face to face. His reputation benefited accordingly.

THE LOUSY LISTENER

"I like to listen. I have learned a great deal from listening carefully. Most people never listen."

ERNEST HEMINGWAY

Bad listeners are like old-fashioned desk blotters. They soak up everything but get it all backwards. You might be tempted to nail one of their feet to the floor just to get their attention.

When dealing with fast-talking lousy listeners, slow the pace of your speech. They'll usually slow down, too.

Lousy listeners start talking before you're even finished because what *they're* going to say is much more important! So they barge in and talk right over you with all the finesse of a pit bull after a mailman.

The end result is that neither of you understands what the other said. When you're giving important information or instructions to a lousy listener, this tendency creates serious misunderstandings and information gaps.

If nothing else, lousy listeners can provide a source of amusement. Their poor listening habits make them prone to malapropisms—using the almost-right word instead of the right word. Lousy listening shows up not only in what people say, but also in what they write. Here are some classics I've either heard or read over the years from students, co-workers, friends, and strangers alike:

- "Let me draw you a diaphragm."
- "When I worked for Fotomat, I spent the whole day sitting inside a little concubine."
- "For all intensive purposes."
- "Needles to say."
- "Let's not circumvent the wheel."
- "Last month's placement report shows that one former prisoner was reincarnated."
- "The fire department's new truck has a heavy-duty wench on the front bumper."
- "Our work team has excellent esprit decor."

Managing Lousy Listeners

1. Speak slowly and deliberately. This will likely be a sharp contrast to the lousy listener, who tends to rattle on at top speed like a hyperactive auctioneer.

Abruptly shifting your speech pattern is the oral equivalent of the "mirroring" behavior that I suggest as a tactic for managing time bombs in a few pages. Since people often subconsciously adopt the same rate of speech as the person they're talking to, your controlled, measured pace may influence the lousy listener to inadvertently slow down his rapid-fire delivery to match your own.

2. Consider such moderating comments or requests as:

- "Either you talk or I'll talk, but we both can't talk at the same time. That won't get us anywhere."

- "The information I just gave you is important. Will you summarize it for me so I'm sure you understood? We can't afford any mistakes."
- "When we talk over each other, neither of us learns anything. You seem to have lots to say, so go ahead. I'll listen carefully. But when it's my turn, I want you to do the same." (Such a "your turn/my turn" technique is especially useful when you want to have the last word, as when giving important instructions or conducting a disciplinary conference.)

3. If lousy listeners work for you, hold them responsible for problems or errors caused by sloppy listening habits.

4. If the lousy listener is your boss, confirm important oral information in a memo so he or she got your message both ways and has a hard-copy record. This time-honored CYA technique can be your best insurance against misunderstandings and confusion.

5. When dealing with critical procedures or step-by-step instructions, ask lousy listeners to confirm their understanding in writing to acknowledge that the directives were received, understood, and will be followed.

THE GIFTED LONER

"Great talents are the most lovely and often the most dangerous fruits on the tree of humanity. They hang upon the most slender twigs that are easily snapped off."

C. G. JUNG

Gifted loners are often very good at what they do. They know it. You know it. Nevertheless, they can be irritating, especially when they work in team-based organizations. Loners are often introverted, sometimes territorial, and frequently temperamental. Their motto might be, "Slide my lunch under the door and leave me alone."

But because these lone wolves are such *valuable* lone wolves, it's necessary to find a suitable niche for them. Or you can try to get them to modify their independent behavior enough to be a compatible fit in their present jobs.

Managing Gifted Loners

1. Ask yourself if this isolationist behavior is typical for the employee in question. Formerly outgoing workers who suddenly become withdrawn and reclusive may be having personal or job-related problems that you're not aware of. If that's the case, this person might benefit from counseling through your company's employee assistance program.

2. In addition, review the employee's work record and accomplishments for the past few months. Have you treated lightly or overlooked outstanding performance or exceptional achieve-

Best Tip

Accommodate gifted loners whenever you can. Their skills will serve you well.

ments? It's common for people who haven't received the praise and recognition they deserve to become resentful and interact as little as possible with management ("You don't appreciate me, so to hell with you.").

If this is the case, meet privately with the person, acknowledge your oversight, apologize (which confirms your commitment to be a fair and honest boss), and set the record straight with a plaque, letter of recognition, or other appropriate gesture—which may be what the worker expected all along. Better late than never.

3. Review the employee's personnel file for skills and abilities that you may have underutilized or ignored. These may qualify him or her for a transfer to a position that requires fewer human relations skills—which might suit some talented loners perfectly.

4. Delegate tasks and projects that the employee can do independently or that don't require much interaction with colleagues. Loners may be the ideal choice for researching prob-

lems, checking out potential solutions, or handling other assignments that don't call for team interaction or collaborative effort.

THE TIME BOMB

"We boil at different degrees."

RALPH WALDO EMERSON

Time bombs have Jekyll-and-Hyde personalities. Treating them
casually can be as dangerous as juggling nitroglycerin or playing
Russian Roulette with a bazooka.

When triggered, time bombs may pitch a full-blown, desk-
pounding, apoplectic fit and create a scene (complete with loud
and profane language) to try to humiliate, bully, or embarrass
you into giving them what they want. They've continued with
and increased the intensity of the tantrums they were probably
allowed to get away with as children. Where's corporal punish-
ment when you need it?

Managing Time Bombs

1. Treat time bombs with discretion, but not deference. The
fact that some co-workers kowtow to time bombs to avoid a
scene only encourages their irritating behavior. Don't join that
crowd.

2. Do not, under any circumstances, show that you're intimidated by a time bomb's tantrums. Once a time bomb sees you're
on the defensive, he or she will go for your throat.

In fact, some time bombs cultivate a loudmouthed and volatile image as a way to hold others at bay and work without
interruptions. So maintain steady eye contact; speak in an even,
well-modulated voice; and don't back down. Time bombs who
are bullies and spoiled brats at heart may change their behavior
abruptly if you show them you're not impressed.

3. Use "mirroring" to try to alter the time bomb's behavior.
Don't lose your cool and be lured into a shouting match; that's
sinking to the time bomb's level, and it shows that the time

bomb has bested you. Instead, you might lower your voice, adopt a casual body posture, or sit down in a chair and see if the time bomb follows suit. If she screams, reply softly and firmly. If he waves his arms and carries on, lean back and cross your legs.

Your behavior is such a marked contrast that it makes the histrionic time bomb look (and, it's hoped, feel) all the more ridiculous. If that happens, the time bomb may begin reflecting your calmer, more rational demeanor—and then you're one step closer to a more rational discussion.

4. If the time bomb is a co-worker, confirm your common interest. Since you're both on the same payroll, at least you can assume that you both want your organization to succeed—which is one starting point for rational discussion and cooperation. Time bombs have little reason to work compatibly with adversaries, so avoid an adversary's role.

Use words like "we," "our," and "us," which imply unity, collaboration, and joint effort. Avoid words like "you" or "I," which tend to make the two of you sound like opponents or antagonists.

5. If the time bomb is an outraged customer, listen carefully, nod supportively, and encourage more

|*Best* Tip

Under no circumstances should you show time bombs special deference. It only encourages them—and undermines your authority.

dialogue with remarks like "I understand," "Tell me more," "I'm listening," "I want to help," and "I can imagine how you feel."

Angry people often need to vent their anger, and as they do, you can sometimes watch them deflate like an overstressed balloon. Once they've got the problem off their chests, they may settle down so you can summarize the complaint or problem succinctly and develop a plan of action to resolve it.

6. If you're negotiating with a time bomb on a mutually beneficial project, employ basic personal selling techniques. How will this person benefit from going along with your proposal? What's in it for her?

Time bombs may be even more explosive if they think they're being conned or manipulated, so it's important to establish that you're bringing a win-win proposition to the table. (One country-boy time bomb I worked with often snarled at would-be manipulators, "Don't pee on my leg and tell me it's raining.")

7. Without appearing whiny, frustrated, or inept, enlist the help of your boss to go over the head of a time bomb who's above your level and stonewalling your progress.

Describe your conflict with the time bomb clearly, why the time bomb's behavior has jeopardized operations, what actions you've taken to manage the person, how he or she reacted, and what changes the time bomb must make to restore a productive and respectful working relationship.

| **Best Tip**

With time bombs, stay cool and be sure not to act intimidated. They love to throw people off balance with their outbursts.

Portray this person's conduct as a roadblock that's retarding the success and profitability of your organization—an obstacle that must be eliminated. If the time bomb reports to one of your boss's peers or is at the same level as your manager, this may be your only recourse if the two of you have reached a stalemate.

8. Try to identify what detonates a time bomb. Does this person tend to explode over certain pet peeves, sensitive subjects, bad news, or in some particular location? If so, you can at least anticipate the explosion and run for cover.

I once asked myself this question about a time bomb I worked with and realized that most of his explosions took place in his office. He apparently didn't like to make a scene or lose control when he wasn't on his home turf. Armed with that knowledge, I started meeting him on neutral ground whenever possible. There, his tantrums were few and far between.

9. If you've managed to set off a time bomb and things have escalated to the shouting stage, say, "I'm willing to discuss this

calmly whenever you settle down. We can talk later." Then turn your back and leave. One caveat, though. Let the nature of the controversy be your guide. Don't walk away if it will make you look like you've been intimidated or are running from a fight. That would only prompt the time bomb to assume he's won the day.

10. If you feel a time bomb is actually a psychotic (see chapter two) who's genuinely capable of "going postal" or threatening physical harm, consider taping one of the outbursts for future reference. A pocket-sized tape recorder in a slightly open desk drawer will do. (Check with an attorney to make sure your state law permits this.)

If circumstances warrant, you may even consider telling the person that you're recording the discussion, which serves notice that you're prepared to take some formal action if things get out of hand. (Of course, this could really—excuse the pun—trigger a violent reaction, so proceed with caution.)

In every case, criticize the *behavior*, not the person. Confirm that you want to work successfully with the time bomb, and voice your hope that the two of you can resolve any conflicts. Time bombs sometimes act the way they do because they feel unappreciated, so a little attention and honest praise can keep them from going off.

THE STEAMROLLER

"Never let the other fellow set the agenda."

JAMES BAKER

Look out! Steamrollers will run you down if you let them. Such colleagues, who are authorities in their field (or who've convinced themselves they are), can be especially irritating because they've got the weight of their ego, if not their credentials, behind them. This only makes them harder to control. And speaking of control, steamrollers *can* be controlled, but only if you're in the driver's seat. No surprise, eh?

Famous for their damn-the-torpedoes behavior, steamrollers are often a toxic combination of other irritating people, especially know-it-alls and lousy listeners—perhaps with a touch of the genetic jerk thrown in. They assume that no one will have the nerve to challenge them and/or everybody thinks they're wonderful and will be delighted to do things their way (heaven help you if you're not).

Steamrollers aren't volatile like time bombs. They have a stable temperament. That is, they're consistently presumptuous, pushy control freaks who'll flatten you if you let them. With steamrollers, you have to cut your own slack, battle for your right to disagree or say no, demand the right to express your opinion, and declare your freedom to exercise your own judgment. They won't make it easy for you; it'll be an uphill battle all the way.

I had a relative like that. A genuinely gifted artist, she naturally assumed that everyone would be delighted to have one of her paintings—no ifs, ands, or buts. And if the people she gave them to objected in the least to the colors, scene, or anything else about it, she was astonished and deeply offended. Hey, this was *her* work! You'd better be humble and grateful to have it, or else!

Managing Steamrollers

1. Without being excessively loud or profane, stand up to steamrollers as you would to any other overbearing bully. They tend to interpret tact and diplomacy as weakness and may test you to see how far they can go. It's okay to be assertive and forceful, because stopping a steamroller usually requires some effort.

Keep a cordial tone of voice and wear a neutral expression, however, so you won't seem overly aggressive. Once you've stood toe-to-toe and earned a steamroller's respect, however, he or she may treat you civilly from that point on.

2. If you make a mistake while working for a steamroller boss, admit it and try to correct it. Denials or lame excuses only make steamrollers gain momentum.

3. Be ready to confirm your position and reinforce your feelings over and over and over again. Because steamrollers are awful listeners who habitually ignore other people, you've got to hang in there and keep hammering away until your message finally breaks through the steamroller's barrier of words and sinks in.

Get in the habit of repeating such phrases as, "Like I said before . . .", "I want to say once again . . .", "I want to make certain that you understand . . .","Let me say for the (umpteenth) time," "Please listen to what I'm saying . . .", and "I'm going to restate my feelings about this. . . ."

|**B**est **T**ip

Dig in and stand your ground with steamrollers. They need to understand that they don't have a lock on all the good ideas.

4. Personalize your discussion by using the steamroller's name often. This helps to assert your conversation's individual nature and keeps your dialogue on a more cordial level.

5. Ask the steamroller to confirm—in writing, if necessary—any decisions and actions you two have agreed on. If you don't, he or she may forget (either accidentally or on purpose) and barge ahead in typical loose-cannon fashion.

THE GADFLY

> *"The right to be heard does not include the right to be taken seriously."*
>
> HUBERT HUMPHREY

Gadflies may be a cross between saboteurs and jolly jokers. They often show traits of both. They tend to be quick-witted and have a gallery of admirers who like to watch them stir things up and are always ready to cheer them on.

Agile managers realize that gadflies can actually be beneficial. They may point out valid flaws in your premises, decisions, objectives, strategies, and management style that you need to re-think and repair.

Try not to dismiss them as just another boil on the butt of tranquillity. At the same time, though, gadflies can certainly be contentious. Their barbs can easily turn venomous if they're not managed with care; it may not take much to turn a relatively inoffensive gadfly into a full-blown saboteur.

Best Tip

Use the natural contrariness in gadflies to identify the flaws in your thinking.

My most memorable gadfly colleague was an ex-army colonel who relished kicking sacred cows. While he had our organization's best interests at heart and volunteered for many committee assignments, he also wrote an occasional underground newsletter in which he lampooned various ill-conceived policies, procedures, and management decisions.

At times he got a bit too vocal for higher management's liking but to management's credit, it didn't overreact. On balance, he was a healthy and constructive presence.

Managing Gadflies

1. Don't go on the offensive. Swatting gadflies only turns them into martyrs. Co-workers will feel sorry for them, and you'll be seen as the bad guy ("The boss really came down on Smedley with golf shoes, didn't he? She didn't deserve to be treated that way.").

That kind of sympathy helps the gadfly expand his power base and circle of admirers. Moreover, attacking the gadfly makes you look insecure. You let that person yank your chain and get under your skin.

2. Involve gadflies in your department's operations so they see why things have to be done as they are. If they understand your reasons and motives, they're less likely to criticize you un-

justifiably or make sweeping indictments of higher managers in general.

3. Ask for their input on key decisions—along with that of everyone else, of course. Not doing so implies you're intimidated by them or have something to hide. This can fuel a gadfly's curiosity and determination even more.

4. If a gadfly turns out to be right about an issue, admit it. Yes, this calls for a very big person. It's tough to do, and lesser managers lack the character. But there will be times in your career (you may have had some already) when reconsidering a decision or admitting a mistake can earn you enormous respect. This makes you the antithesis of the stereotypical pig-headed manager whose motto might be, "I may not be right, but I'm never wrong."

THE WHINER

"When I hear somebody sigh, 'Life is hard,' I am always tempted to ask, 'Compared to what?' "

SYDNEY HARRIS

Whiners think it's them against the world. They're helpless victims . . . pawns in life's chess game . . . overwhelmed by circumstances beyond their control. They believe in the tongue-in-cheek motto, "Somewhere, someone is having a meeting to decide your future and you weren't invited!"

Aside from feeling like the world's doormat, some whiners may bellyache because they've set exceedingly high performance standards and things didn't turn out as well as they'd hoped. Whatever the reason, whiners who are left unmanaged will continue to be part of the problem instead of part of the solution. Anybody can complain about a situation, but it usually takes hard work to make it better.

Like some other forms of irritating behavior, whining can become contagious. When one pup in the litter starts whining, the rest often join in—and pandemonium reigns. (What's the difference between a whiner and a puppy? The puppy stops whining after it grows up!)

I recall another co-worker who complained about *everything*. He reminded me of Joe Bfstplk in the Li'l Abner cartoon— perpetually trudging around under a dark cloud. There was always something wrong. His whining got so bad that the rest of us never asked him how he was doing, because he was sure to tell us—and we'd all end up feeling depressed, put upon, overworked, and generally dumped on.

Managing Whiners

1. Listen carefully. Although giving whiners an audience encourages them to keep on whining, a whiner may sometimes have a legitimate complaint. If you ignore it, it could turn into a full-fledged morale problem and a grievance filed with higher management. Even perpetual whiners have a valid case once in a while. This could be one.

2. Call the whiner's bluff. Sometimes people whine out of boredom, to attract attention, or just to hear themselves. If you suspect that's the case, ask the person frankly, "Tell me what the problem seems to be and exactly what you want me to do." Those who are just blowing smoke won't be able to produce a legitimate gripe or specific suggestions. With any luck, this direct approach may shut them up.

Best Tip
Manage whiners carefully. Like worrywarts, they can spread their aggravating behavior to other members of the work group.

3. Challenge the word "unfair." It's popular with whiners, and they tend to use it generically to mean "not getting whatever I want." When a whiner complains about "unfair" treatment, press for specific examples. What seems to be unfair about

the situation? In what way? Would responding to this person's claim make you "unfair" to other people in your department? (Note: keeping a record of work assignments and delegated tasks helps you distribute the load equitably and avoid claims that you've been "unfair.")

4. Remind whiners that it's often necessary to compromise and make the most of a bad situation. Some of them may have unrealistic demands or expect you to work miracles just to send them away happy. Well, life isn't always perfect, and democratic management has its limits. A reality check may be in order.

A friend of mine who owned a successful auto dealership had to do some painful downsizing. Naturally, this increased the workload for everyone who was left, including his bookkeeper, who had a tendency to whine.

When he met with her one day to tell her about some new additions to her job description, she said, "I simply can't take on any more work. I'm overloaded already; there's no *way* I'd be able to do these things too."

Best Tip

Call a whiner's bluff by confronting the person directly: "What's the problem? What can I do to help the situation?"

He looked at her, nodded sympathetically, and said, "I understand your situation, but I'm awfully sorry to hear you say that. I really need somebody who can carry a heavier load. Can you recommend a replacement?"

She stammered, stuttered, mentally reviewed the implications of his question, and said that, well, maybe, on second thought, she might be able to handle these new tasks after all.

5. If you're a team leader, whiners can be hazardous to the health of your group. Perpetual complainers disrupt a team's harmony and cohesiveness and may even promote group whining—which is the last thing you need. So it may be necessary to arrange a transfer for, or even to replace, congenital whiners who refuse to get with the program.

6. Focus on solutions, not problems. Make it a habit to ask whiners, "What do you think we should do about it?"

This tactic has at least two benefits. First, it makes whiners realize that they can't just dump a problem in your lap and disappear down the hall. You expect them to have produced some possible solutions as well. Second, it will motivate whiners to whine less, because you're not all that sympathetic. As word gets out that you expect them to think through problems and create some ready solutions before coming to you, they'll tend to think for themselves more and involve you less.

7. Team up whiners with self-sufficient, resourceful co-workers who will serve as good role models. Be careful, however. This might backfire. It's possible that your model employees could be influenced by the whiner's behavior and join the chorus, which is the opposite of what you intended. You could end up with a handful of bad apples instead of just one.

8. Give whiners a process or scheme for attacking problems. Sometimes people whine because they're stymied. They don't know how to get their arms around a problem, frame it up, put it in focus, and develop a plan of attack. So they sit and moan and fuss, become more and more frustrated, and sometimes hope that if they carry on loudly and long enough, you'll jump in like a swivel-chair Superman and make all the bad things go away. A brief seminar in problem-solving or creative thinking, then, may fill this gap in the whiner's skill set.

9. Refuse to commiserate. Misery loves company, so empathy only reinforces a whiner's behavior. Try to turn the conversation in other directions with comments like, "I refuse to see things that way" or "Griping isn't going to do us any good; let's change the subject."

10. As a last resort, you may have to simply tell the whiner to knock it off and get on with life. The constant complaining is screwing up the work and the work group and has gone far enough. Diplomacy and tact have their limits.

The Agile Manager's Checklist

Cynical Old-Timers

✔ Take advantage of their value as resources.

✔ Recruit them as allies.

✔ Do your homework first before debating them.

✔ Ask for their support and tell them why.

Patronizers

✔ Deal with patronizers head on.

Information Misers

✔ Lay a paper trail that documents your requests for information in case you have to go over their heads.

✔ Keep a record of their typical roadblocks, excuses, and delays.

Saboteurs

✔ Broadcast your successes to offset a saboteur's sniping.

✔ Radiate self-confidence: head high, shoulders back, and steady as she goes.

✔ Choose your words carefully whenever they're around.

Lousy Listeners

✔ Speak slowly and deliberately.

✔ Hold lousy-listener employees responsible for the consequences of their poor listening habits.

✔ Confirm important oral information given to a lousy-listener boss in writing

Gifted Loners

✔ Review recent performance; praise achievements that you may have overlooked.

✔ Consider arranging a transfer to a position that requires fewer human relations skills.

Time Bombs

✔ Refuse to act intimidated.

✔ Show them how they'll benefit from doing what you want.

✔ Identify the things that set them off so you can anticipate and perhaps avoid an explosion.

Checklist, continued

Steamrollers

✔ Earn their respect by standing up to them.

✔ Confirm your position and state your feelings repeatedly.

✔ Call them by name to keep the discussion personal.

✔ Ask them to confirm any decisions or actions you've agreed upon to keep them on course.

Gadflies

✔ Don't discipline or reprimand them harshly.

✔ Involve them in projects that will show them why things must be done as they are.

✔ Ask for their input on key decisions.

✔ Admit when they're right to earn their respect and demonstrate your depth of character.

Whiners

✔ Be willing to admit that their complaints might be justified.

✔ Demand examples of alleged "unfair" treatment.

✔ Match a whiner with co-workers who can be positive role models.

✔ Don't commiserate; it only encourages them.

✔ When all else fails, tell them to stop whining and get on with the job.

Chapter Four

Look in the Mirror: Who's Really Irritating?

*"Oh would some power the gift to give us
To see ourselves as others see us
It would from many a blunder free us
And foolish notion"*

ROBERT BURNS

"So that's how it went," the Agile Manager said to Anita. "My words seemed to have a deeper impact on him than I thought they would. Do you think I was too hard?"

"He did some a little shell shocked the rest of the day," said Anita, "but he came in the next day with the sunniest disposition I've ever seen for him. He was like that the next day too—and uniformly helpful to everyone. He really does have some good skills, especially for a project like this one. Anyway, the whole team has brightened up too, so I'm not about to criticize the way you handled the situation."

"Good. But as long as we're talking in this vein, I've noticed that Bobby and Janet both seem to shrink in my presence. Do you know why that is? If it's the way I act, I'd really like to know. I ask *because it's irritating—I want to know what they're thinking—I want to know them, and I can't seem to get them to come out of their shells."*

She bit her lip briefly, then said, "Bobby jokes all day long. I'd never considered him a turtle! I know you. When you're thinking about something, you close into your own world and keep most other people out. I know how to get in when you're like that, and I know you don't mind being called back into the team's reality. But I doubt the newcomers do. You probably appear forbidding to them. They think you'll get mad, I bet, if they talk to you. And so they may be afraid."

The Agile Manager appeared thoughtful for a moment, then said, "That's great feedback Anita—thanks for being honest. I know just what to do with that information."

As the dentist said when he ran out of Lidocaine, "Hold on. This is going to hurt a little." Introspection often does. And while it's never much fun to do exploratory surgery on your psyche, understand that it's possible *you* could be at fault—perhaps just a tiny bit—for some of the irritating behavior that's been bugging you at work.

Seeing yourself objectively, however, is hard to do. Imagine you're a buzzard dining on fresh road kill. To you, your behavior is normal if not exemplary. Onlookers, however, may want to throw up. So how can you step outside your own gilt-edged frame of reference and try to see yourself through the eyes of co-workers who may, in fact, believe *you're* a pain in the neck? Here are a few suggestions.

Best Tip
Don't ask people at work to critique your personality. The request may be misinterpreted by the person you ask.

Ask Acquaintances for Input

Note that this says "acquaintances," not "friends." "A friend," it has been said, "is somebody who knows all your faults but

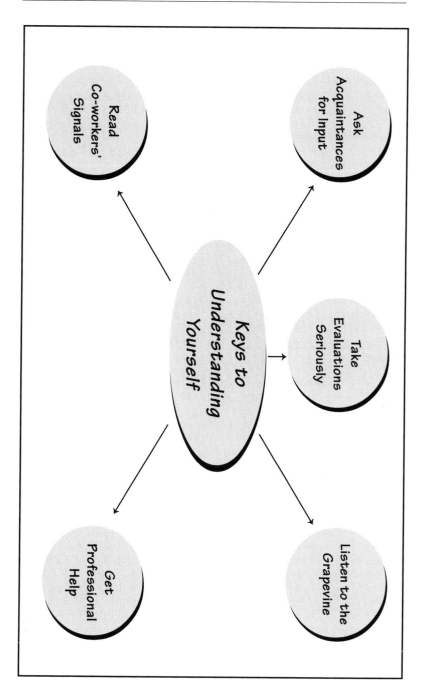

Keys to Understanding Yourself

- Read Co-workers' Signals
- Ask Acquaintances for Input
- Take Evaluations Seriously
- Get Professional Help
- Listen to the Grapevine

likes you anyway." And someone who really is your friend is likely to shine you on when you ask for an honest opinion. But if you approach them properly and explain the reasons behind your request, acquaintances who have known you casually for several years may open some windows to your behavior that you yourself have kept tightly closed.

It's not a good idea to make this request of acquaintances at work for at least two good reasons.

First, they might someday end up reporting to you. Second, you might someday end up reporting to *them!* In either case, your earlier request to "level with me" could turn out to be embarrassing. It might be construed as a lack of confidence, insecurity, or instability, none of which would help your reputation very much.

So it's best to talk to nonworking acquaintances—people you routinely meet and have good rapport with at your health club, in your golf foursome, country club, or civic groups, and those you've known for several years as members of service clubs or professional organizations.

Best Tip

Heed your performance evaluations. They can be excellent sources of feedback about your irritating behavior.

This doesn't have to be a soul-bearing, let-it-all-hang-out, spill-your-guts emotional encounter, for gosh sakes. You might solicit some opinions (and yes, the predictable wisecracks, all in good fun, let's hope) with prompting comments such as:

- "Lately I've been looking at how I come across to other people. Sort of a self-improvement kick. Since you know me fairly well, what have you noticed that I might do better somehow for the sake of my career? I'm really serious—I'd appreciate your comments."
- "Sometimes I wonder what I could do to get people at

work to be more open with me and tell me what's on their minds. I'm not sure they're doing that now, and maybe it's my fault. What do you suggest?"

■ "We've known each other for quite a while now, and I'd like to ask your opinion. I'm reviewing my career strategy and personal-development plan. What things might I do to help me work more effectively with other people?"

Take Performance Evaluations Seriously

If you have a forthright boss, some of your more irritating behavior may already have cropped up on your performance evaluations. Any behavior that's irritating your boss needs to be addressed ASAP, of course, but it's equally important to resolve conduct that's impairing your effectiveness with peers and subordinates alike. Left untended, such things will have a negative ripple effect throughout your sphere of influence.

Best Tip

Take the grapevine's feedback with a grain of salt, but admit to yourself that it could be on target.

Listen to the Grapevine

What do people say about you when you're not around? The grapevine will carry this information through various channels, including secretaries' gossip, coffee-lounge comments, and even restroom graffiti.

Granted, this information should be carefully filtered, because saboteurs and others of their ilk are only too glad to stab you in the back. But don't chalk up every unflattering thing you hear about yourself to jealousy or some crackpot's opinion. Admit to the possibility that some of the remarks might be accurate and justified.

Read Co-workers' 'Signals'

What signals do people send that indicate they feel uncomfortable or irritated with you? Look for some of these clues from peers and subordinates alike:

- They avoid or minimize contact with you. This may include, for example, poor eye contact during conversations, answering your questions evasively, canceling out of your meetings or sending a delegate if possible, following a traffic pattern that deliberately detours around your office and other places where you're usually found, and sending written or voice-mail messages when a face-to-face discussion would obviously be more convenient.
- They keep opinions or ideas to themselves, or they volunteer them only when pressured. Reluctant, clam-like behavior may indicate that they consider you a steamroller, know-it-all, or time bomb, just to name a few.
- They are overly deferential to you or agree with everything you say. When two people agree on everything, one of them usually isn't doing much thinking. Employees who would agree that it's raining Beefeater Gin just because you say so may have been verbally flayed when they disagreed with you in the past and swore never to make that mistake again. Agile managers seek out and cultivate confident, competent employees who make valuable contributions to the group by speaking their minds without fear of reprisal. Are *your* people willing to do so?

Best Tip

If people are avoiding you, find out why. The answer just may save your career.

Get Professional Help

A trained professional may be able to help you analyze and understand yourself much more effectively than you ever could hope to do on your own. Such folks may range from a personal career coach to a psychologist paid for by your company's employee assistance program.

In addition to providing objective professional guidance about how to recognize and change counterproductive behavior patterns, professionals may also recommend a number of assessment tests to help you:

Best Tip

Try a self-assessment test. It can help you put a label on your personality type and your reactions to people and situations.

- Put your personality type and behavior or learning style in sharp focus.
- Understand the process you usually follow when making decisions and dealing with routine situations at work.
- Improve your self-knowledge, your ability to relate to others, and how you're likely to respond in certain working environments.

Three of the more widely known are:

Kolb's Learning Style Inventory. Describes how you process ideas and respond to situations that you encounter at work based on four types of learning styles: Accommodators, Divergers, Convergers, and Assimilators.

Myers-Briggs Type Indicator. Helps to clarify your preferred approach to making decisions and working with others by asking you to choose preferred alternatives based on four sets of opposites: Extroversion/Introversion, Sensing/Intuition, Thinking/Feeling, and Judging/Perceiving.

The results can give you insight into how people with different personality styles can communicate more effectively and employ the relative strengths of their respective personalities to work together successfully.

Gregoric Style Delineator. Although similar to Myers-Briggs, this instrument tends to assess a different set of preferences and

Best Tip

Although quick and easy, online assessment tests are no substitute for advice from qualified professionals.

identify which of four channels you tend to use when learning new information: Concrete Random, Concrete Sequential, Abstract Random, or Abstract Sequential. Knowing your preferred learning channel may help you reduce naiveté, become more responsible for your thoughts and actions, and improve how you work with others.

The Internet has an assortment of interesting Web sites that offer self-analysis and assessment tests, too. Of course, it should go without saying that cyberanalysis is no substitute for one-on-one sessions with a personal coach or counselor. Nevertheless, online tests may give you an inkling of what makes you tick and why. What you do with that inkling is up to you, of course. Just be sure to feed and water it often.

www.psychtests.com/tests.html

This site has loads of online tests developed by Cyberia Shrink. Some of the ones that are closely connected to the theme of this book are:

PERSONALITY TESTS

- Depression Inventory
- Sales Personality Inventory
- Extroversion/Introversion Inventory
- Type A Inventory
- Self-Esteem Inventory
- Social Anxiety Test
- Anxiety Inventory

INTELLIGENCE TESTS

- Emotional Intelligence ("life-smart") Test
- Coping Skills Inventory (Assesses how you react to stress)
- Assertiveness Inventory

- Communication Skills Inventory

ATTITUDE, LIFESTYLE, AND EMOTIONAL HEALTH TESTS

- Arguing Style Inventory
- Optimism/Pessimism Inventory
- Burnout Inventory

www.queendom.com/test_frm.html

This is The Body-Mind QueenDom's Test Collection. It contains links to various tests on the WWW *not* developed by Cyberia Shrink. They include:

PERSONALITY TESTS

- Mental and Emotional Health Assessment
- General Health and Lifestyle Assessment
- Attitude
- Career Choice and Preparation

www.onlinepsych.com/public/Mind_Games/list.htm#P1

This site, Mind Games at Online Psych, has a variety of challenging, informative, and amusing tests, including:

PERSONALITY TESTS

- Self-esteem
- Assertiveness
- Extrovert/Introvert Personality Assessment
- Type A Personality
- Sales Personality

MENTAL HEALTH SCREENING TESTS

- Depression Screening Test
- Depression Inventory
- Online Screening For Anxiety
- Anxiety Personality Type Questionnaire
- Personality Disorder Screening Test
- Social Anxiety Screening Test

The typical disclaimer on these sites emphasizes that the tests are intended for informational purposes only. They're not meant to substitute for psychological and medical advice from qualified professionals and don't claim to offer psychological or medical treatment. If you need psychological or medical evaluation or treatment, go to a qualified professional.

You Gotta Wanna

This chapter's suggestions for getting to know yourself will only work if you believe they're worthwhile and you're motivated to use them. You need to have the "want to," not the "I wish I could." If you suspect that some of your behavior is detrimental and counterproductive to your career and/or personal relationships, chances are you're right. But no one can *really* set the wheels of change in motion except you.

Understand that you'll only resolve to change your behavior if your security or serenity is threatened.

Some twenty years ago, business consultant Lonnie Fitzgerald told me, "People only change when their security or serenity are threatened." I've thought about his observation many times since then, and try as I might, I've never found any holes in it.

If you're content doing business as usual and following your standard pattern of behavior (which, we've already acknowledged, may be just fine), then go for it.

But if you employ several of the feedback devices suggested here and they indicate that you're responsible for many of your problems at work, then the odds are you're overdue for a self-imposed behavior overhaul. And while this is admittedly a major revelation (as easy for some, perhaps, as a leopard changing its spots), the effort, time, and final results can literally change the quality and direction of your life, and the lives of those close to you, for the better.

Agile managers are always on the lookout for ways to do that.

The Agile Manager's Checklist

✔ Ask personal acquaintances to suggest how you might improve your on-the-job relationships.
✔ Take seriously any negative traits that surface on your performance evaluations.
✔ Get feedback from the grapevine about traits that rub others the wrong way.
✔ Watch for co-workers' clues that reveal they're not comfortable around you.
✔ Find a career coach or psychologist to help you understand your behavior constructively and objectively.
✔ Use assessment tests to give you insight to behavioral patterns and traits that you probably aren't aware of.
✔ Remember: no one can change your irritating behavior except you.

Index